Colette's Wedding Cakes

Also by Colette Peters

Colette's Christmas
Colette's Cakes

Colette's Wedding Cakes

COLETTE PETERS

Photographs by Colin Cooke

LITTLE, BROWN AND COMPANY

BOSTON   NEW YORK   TORONTO   LONDON

Library of Congress Cataloging-in-Publication Data

Peters, Colette.
    Colette's wedding cakes / Colette Peters ; photographs by Colin
Cooke. — 1st ed.
        p.   cm.
    ISBN 0-316-70256-0
    I. Cake decorating.   2. Wedding cakes.   I. Title.
TX771.2.P48   1995
641.8′653 — dc20
                                                            94-5299

10 9 8 7 6 5 4 3 2 I

KP

Published simultaneously in Canada
by Little, Brown & Company (Canada) Limited

Printed in the United States of America

Contents

Acknowledgments

I would like to thank the following people for all of their help and generosity.
I could never have written this book without them!

Colin Cooke

Wendy Kromer

Margot Abel

Jennifer Josephy

Angela Miller

Karen and Chris Tack

The McCoys

David Lo

Robert Bacall

and, of course, Puppet Boy

The Art of the Wedding Cake

Wedding cakes are a joyous tradition around the world. In many cultures, some type of decorated confection is served to symbolize fertility and luck, and to allow well-wishers to share the good fortune of the happy couple. The art of the wedding cake reached its pinnacle in the stylized sentiment of the Victorian era. The visual style, materials, and decorating techniques of today's wedding cakes evolved from the Victorians' view of love, as well as their love of ornament.

According to confectionary tradition, wedding cakes in the United States are butter or sponge cake, and the top tier is frozen until the couple's first anniversary. One wedding-cake custom, however, has changed dramatically: The cake no longer has to be all white. Today cakes may be decorated to match the theme, colors, location, and season of the celebration. The decorations may suggest the architectural motifs of an ornate grand ballroom or the setting of a simple wedding on the beach, each having its own special meaning for the bride and groom. Sugar flowers and other ornaments can be sculpted to look so realistic that the cake may be the conversation piece of the wedding, sometimes even overshadowing the bride's gown. And everyone loves to take home a flower from the cake as a cherished memento.

The creation of a beautiful wedding cake requires a certain degree of skill and patience, but there is nothing mysterious about it. A wedding cake, no matter how elaborate, is nothing more than a stack of graduated cakes decorated to create a total effect that matches the couple's style. Starting as an artist with a love of baking, I taught myself the basics of cake decorating from books and through trial and error. Over the years, making cakes has sharpenend both my sense of design and my imagination. Even though I often make fun and challenging cakes for all sorts of occasions, I still feel that designing and executing cakes for weddings is the most exciting and fulfilling part of my profession. My purpose in writing this book is to share my experience as a cake decorator — including the resources I've discovered and the tricks I've developed over the years. Hopefully, the cakes in this book will inspire your confidence in creating unique designs of your own.

The best way to use this book is to read the chapters in the back entitled "Basic Recipes" and "Basic Instructions" before you begin. These chapters explain the tools and materials you will need, as well as how to make the decorations and assemble the cakes. Refer to these chapters as you follow the directions for the cakes, which are organized by season in the first part of the book. The "Basic Recipes" section includes instructions for making rolled fondant and various icings, as well as a chart to help you determine how much fondant you will need to cover a given cake. The amount of icing required for each cake will depend on whether you plan to use it for filling, icing, or decorating, so the directions do not specify quantities. When you make your cake, keep a supply of icing ingredients on hand and make more as you need it. With practice, you'll be able to estimate more easily. When I design a wedding cake, I keep in mind that it represents the celebration of a very special day. I want all of my cakes to contain the elements that I believe every good marriage needs: uniqueness, a sense of humor, and a lot of loving care.

Spring

Stained-Glass Cake

The transparent quality of piping gel gave me the idea of using it to create the look of colored glass. Piping gel can be bought in small tubes of various colors in the grocery store baking section. You can also purchase clear gel from cake decorating suppliers, tint it with liquid food coloring, and pipe it through a pastry bag.

Serves 135

Cakes:
  8-inch round, 3 inches high
  11-inch round, 3 inches high
  14-inch round, 3 inches high
18-inch round base, $\frac{1}{2}$ inch thick
royal icing (page 144)
white glue
$\frac{1}{2}$-inch-wide white ribbon for the edge of the
  base and tiers
8-, 11-, and 14-inch round foamcore boards

rolled fondant (page 142)
$\frac{1}{4}$-inch-thick wooden dowels
brown paste food coloring
clear piping gel and red, yellow, green, blue,
  purple, and pink food coloring OR tubes of
  ready-to-use colored piping gel
pastry bags and couplers
tip #2

In advance:

Cover the base with thinned white royal icing. Let dry. Glue the ribbon around the edge of the base.

To decorate the cake:

Bake the cakes and let them cool completely. Assemble the tiers on their corresponding foamcore boards. Cover with rolled fondant. Insert dowels in the tiers and stack the tiers on the prepared base. Attach ribbon around the edge of each tier with a little royal icing.

Transfer the design onto the cake by placing patterns 1–17 on the cake and outlining them with a long pin. Keep in mind that some of the designs will go over the edge and onto the top of the cake.

Tint some royal icing dark brown. Use a pastry bag with the #2 tip to outline the designs.

If you are using clear piping gel, place about 2 heaping tablespoons of gel in small containers. Add a few drops of food coloring to each container and mix. The gel will appear darker in the container than it will on the cake, so be sure to test each color by spreading a little on some spare fondant. Add more color a drop at a time if necessary.

Fill pastry bags with the different gels and use the #2 tip to pipe the gels into the designs, using the photograph as a guide. If you use tubes of ready-made gel, you can pipe the gel directly into the designs from the tubes.

Patterns 1–17

Edwardian Cake

Bride's magazine commissioned me to design an all-white cake based on the elaborate Edwardian ceiling ornamentation in the Burden Mansion in New York City. Translating the intricacies of the plaster detailing into icing requires many of the decorating techniques I discuss in this book. The result is an exceptionally beautiful cake that recalls the elegance and craftsmanship of a bygone era.

Serves 280

Cakes:
- 5-inch round, 4 inches high
- 8-inch round, 4 inches high
- 12-inch round, 4 inches high
- 16-inch round, 6 inches high

2 sugar molds (page 170):
- I, made in a cup $3\frac{1}{2}$ inches wide by $2\frac{3}{4}$ inches high
- I, made in a tart pan 3 inches wide by I inch high

royal icing (page 144)

3-inch-long Styrofoam egg

wax paper

royal-icing decorations (pages 150–154):
- 40 small rosebuds
- 38 medium roses, 10 of them on stems
- 30 large roses, 10 of them on stems
- 120 small daisies, 10 of them on stems
- 34 medium daisies
- 4 large daisies on stems
- 20 small petunias, 5 of them on stems
- 8 medium petunias on stems
- 20 leaves on stems
- 12 baby's breath on wires

- 80 small and 26 large grape clusters
- 15 grape clusters on wires

gum-paste decorations (pages 155–166):
- 60 small apples, pears, and pumpkins
- 6 shells, made from Wilton Baroque mold kit
- 56 leaves, made with leaf cutter (pages 167–169)

cornstarch

10-inch Styrofoam disk, I inch high

8-inch Styrofoam disk, I inch high

20-inch round base, $\frac{1}{2}$ inch thick

white glue

$\frac{1}{2}$-inch-wide white ribbon to cover edge of base

5-, 8- (use 2), 12-, and 16-inch round foamcore boards

royal buttercream icing (page 139)

$\frac{1}{4}$-inch-thick wooden dowels

toothpicks

pastry bags and couplers

tips #1.5, #2, #3, #10, #14, #18, #22, #44, #45, #65S, #65, #67, #199, and #363

In advance:

Make a hollow sugar mold from the cup and a solid mold from the tart pan. When they are dry, attach the narrow end of the solid mold to the bottom of the cup mold with royal icing to form a vase. Let dry. Attach the 3-inch Styrofoam egg inside the vase with royal icing. To decorate, place the vase on a piece of wax paper and use the #2 tip to pipe royal-icing lines along the vertical ridges of the base. Pipe a shell border around the top of the lines with the #14 tip and another at the bottom with the #18 tip. Let dry.

Make 6 large and 6 small run-in sugar ovals, using patterns I and 2 (see page 12). When the ovals are dry, pipe evenly spaced diagonal lines with the #44 tip on the small ovals in only one direction, then pipe overlapping lines in the other direction. Pipe another layer of diagonal lines over the first 2 sets. Finally,

Figure 2

Roll the gum-paste fruits between $\frac{3}{8}$ inch and $\frac{1}{2}$ inch wide using figure 2 as a guide. Let dry for at least 24 hours.

Next, bevel the 10-inch Styrofoam disk. Use the 8-inch cake pan to mark the top (see the section on Styrofoam, page 174). Cover the beveled edge of the disk with a thin coat of royal icing.

Using royal icing, attach one of the 8-inch round foamcore boards to the bottom of the 8-inch Styrofoam disk. Cover the sides with royal icing, then use royal icing to attach the whole thing to the bottom of the beveled disk.

Cut out and vein the gum-paste leaves. Attach 25 leaves diagonally around the sides of the 8-inch disk. Pipe dots with the #3 tip at the bottom of all of the leaves (figure 3). Attach the remaining leaves upright around the beveled layer, but don't let the tops extend above the edge. The piping around the leaves will be

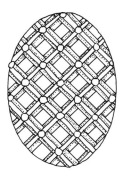

Figure 1

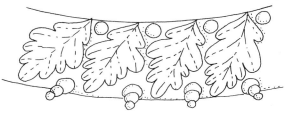

Figure 3

using the #3 tip, pipe another layer of diagonal lines on top. Pipe small dots with the #2 tip at all intersections. Let dry (figure 1).

Make all of the royal-icing flowers, leaves, and grape clusters and let dry. Place the stemmed ones in the vase, piping royal icing from the #18 tip to hold them in place. Use the photograph as a guide.

Make 6 gum-paste shells from the Wilton mold, brushing the mold with a thin coat of shortening before pressing in the paste. Do not include the extension pieces at the sides of the shells. Dust both sides of the shells with cornstarch and let them dry on a concave surface.

decorated after the 8-inch cake is placed on top. Set aside.

Cover the base with thinned royal icing and glue the ribbon around the edge.

To decorate the cake:

Bake the cakes and let them cool completely. Assemble the tiers on their corresponding foamcore boards. Cover the tiers with royal buttercream icing. Insert the dowels. Place the 16-inch tier on the prepared base.

All of the piping on the cake will be done with royal buttercream icing.

Divide the 16-inch tier into 6 equal sections and mark them with a toothpick (see page 173). Mark 3 arcs, each measuring the width of two sections. Pipe the arcs using the #45 tip. Attach a large oval at each of the 6 marks (figure 4). Pipe S-shaped scrolls with the #2 tip along the arcs, facing left on the left side of the ovals and facing right on the right side. Over-

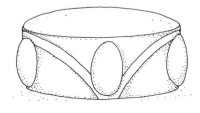

Figure 4

pipe the scrolls with the #1.5 tip. Add small curls to embellish the scrolls. Use the #2 tip to pipe a snail trail above and below the arcs (see page 148). Add a row of dots beneath the snail trail (figure 5).

Pipe a line around the bottom of the tier with the #22 tip. Pipe a reverse shell border over the line.

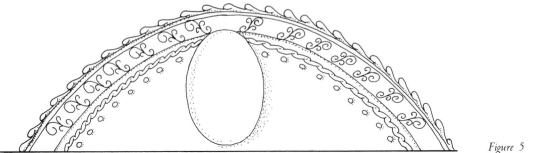

Figure 5

Overpipe the shells with the #3 tip. Pipe a rope border around the contour of the shells with the #2 tip (figure 6). Pipe branches and curls on both sides of the ovals with the #2 tip.

Attach a gum-paste shell at the bottom of each oval, as shown in the photograph. Then attach flowers, grapes, and fruit around the ovals. Fill in with leaves piped with the #65S and #65 tips.

Figure 6

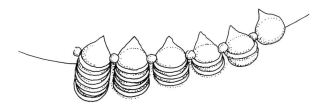

Figure 7

Figure 8

Pipe a dot border on the top edge of the tier with the #10 tip, starting the dot on the edge and ending it toward the center of the cake. With the #2 tip, pipe 5 strings over each dot and finish each with a dot (figure 7).

Place the 12-inch tier on the bottom tier. Divide the tier into 6 sections, matching the marks on the tier below. Attach a lattice oval at each mark.

Pipe 6 garlands between the ovals with the #18 tip, using a slight zigzag motion. Attach flowers, grapes, and fruit. Fill in with piped leaves, using the #65 tip. Pipe trailing branches and curls with the #2 tip, extending from the garlands.

Pipe 6 reverse shells with the #18 tip around the base on each side of the ovals, each facing to the left and right of the center.

Pipe 2 rows of 3 shells below the ovals with the #363 tip (figure 8).

Pipe a border of elongated shells with the #18 tip along the top edge of the tier. With the #2 tip, pipe a snail trail below the shells, following their contour. Above the shell border, pipe a snail trail with the #2 tip around each shell. Pipe dots in front of each shell. Pipe 2 curved trailing lines with the #2 tip toward the center of the cake (figure 9).

Place the 8-inch disk and bevel assembly on top.

Figure 9

Place the 8-inch tier on top of the bevel. Pipe fleurs-de-lis with the #14 tip between the leaves at the intersection of the 8-inch cake and the bevel. Pipe a line of dots with the #3 tip below the fleurs-de-lis (figure 10).

Pipe 7 horizontal ovals around the middle of the tier with the #18 tip, using pattern 3. Attach flowers and grapes to the ovals, then fill in by piping leaves with the #65 tip.

Place the 5-inch tier on top. Pipe 12 scrolls with the #18 tip around the side, starting in the middle of the tier and continuing down to the base. Overpipe

with the #3 tip, then again with the #2 tip. Pipe a line of dots with the #2 tip above the scrolls, following their contours. Pipe a snail trail above the dots with the same tip.

Place one of the 12 large grape clusters at the end of each scroll on top of the 8-inch tier. Between the grapes, pipe a scroll with the #3 tip, extending it slightly over the edge of the tier. Between the scrolls, pipe a ruffled border with the #67 tip around the top edge of the tier. Pipe a leaf with the #67 tip next to

each scroll. Pipe curls with the #2 tip along each scroll (figure 11).

Around the top edge of the 5-inch tier, pipe alternating longer and shorter vertical shells overhanging the edge, using the #199 tip. With the #2 tip, pipe a string across the short shells, then 2 strings across the long ones (figure 12).

When the cake reaches its final destination, attach the sugar vase to the top of the cake with a dab of icing.

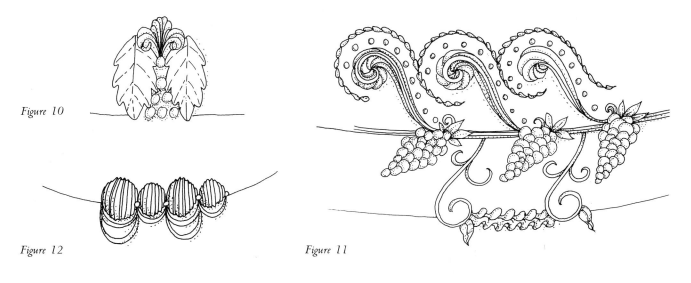

Figure 10

Figure 12

Figure 11

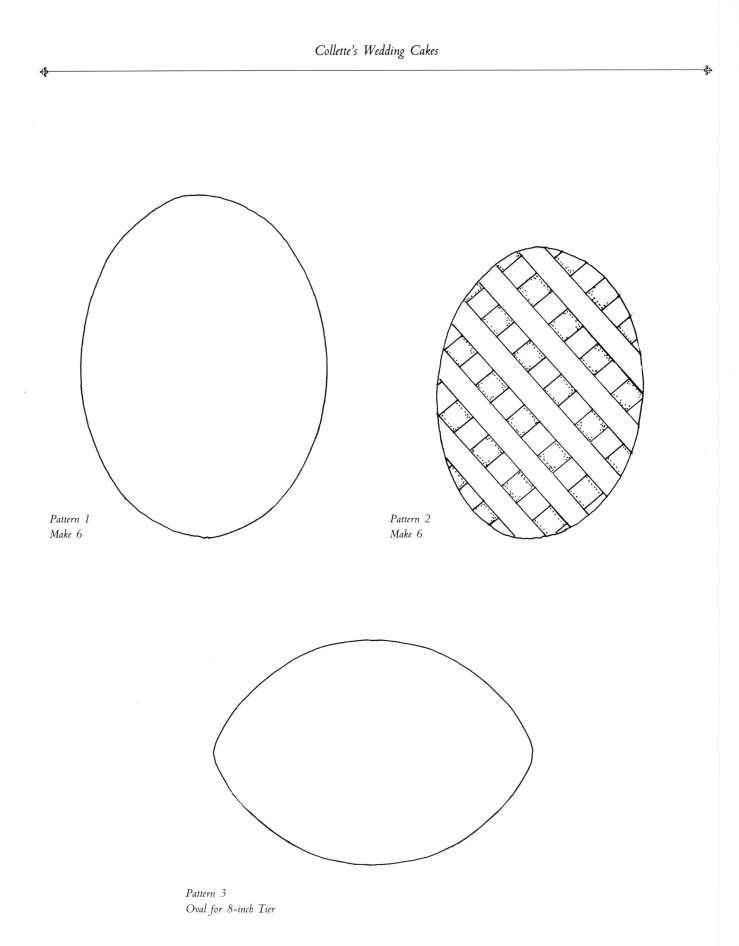

Pattern 1
Make 6

Pattern 2
Make 6

Pattern 3
Oval for 8-inch Tier

Tiers of Joy

This cake was created for a fashion designer, so I borrowed motifs from the world of fashion. I had great fun imitating the look of various fabrics, sewing techniques, types of clothing, and accessories, such as hats, bows, ruffles, and quilting.

Serves 400

❧

Cakes:
- 8-inch round, 3 inches high
- 12-inch petal, 4 inches high
- 14-inch round, 5 inches high
- 18-inch round, 6 inches high

24-inch round base, $\frac{1}{2}$ inch thick

royal icing (page 144)

white glue

$\frac{1}{2}$-inch-wide white ribbon to cover the edge of the base

gum paste (page 155)

gum-paste decorations (pages 155–166):
- 20 pale pink apple blossoms
- 13 pink, white, yellow, and blue apple blossoms on stems
- 8 small green leaves
- 6 fabric roses, $1\frac{1}{2}$ inches wide

25 small pink and red royal-icing roses

paper towels

royal-blue, moss-green, black, purple, orange, and pink paste food coloring

lemon extract

small paintbrushes

4 5-inch columns

hot-glue gun

Styrofoam cone, 6 inches wide at the base and 7 inches high

4-, 8-, 14-, and 18-inch round foamcore boards

12-inch petal-shaped foamcore board

rolled fondant (page 142)

plastic bird

Wilton Baroque gum-paste mold kit

nontoxic yellow, white, and gold iridescent powder

flexible cardboard

X-acto knife

right triangle

tracing wheel

$\frac{1}{4}$-inch-thick wooden dowels

$\frac{1}{4}$- and $\frac{3}{8}$-inch silver dragées

pink powdered coloring

ruler

marshmallows

1-inch circle cutter

$\frac{3}{8}$-inch-wide red ribbon

basic buttercream icing (page 139)

pastry bags and couplers

tips #2, #17, #20, #45, #66, #68, and #127

❧

In advance:

Cover the base with thinned white royal icing. Let dry. Glue ribbon around the edge of the base.

Make all of the gum-paste flowers and leaves. Make the pink and red royal-icing roses. Let dry.

Make 17 2-by-1-inch white gum-paste ribbons with one notched end. Dry them slightly curved on crumpled paper towels. To make the 12 loops, start with a 5-inch strip, 1 inch wide (page 155). Let dry.

When the ribbons and loops are dry, mix black coloring with lemon extract and paint 3 vertical stripes on them with a small brush.

Cut 4 9-by-$\frac{1}{2}$-inch strips of gum paste. Brush water on the back of each strip and wrap one strip around each column. Paint the strips black. Hot-glue the 4 columns, with their bases touching, to the center of the 4-inch foamcore circle. Add a little hot glue to the

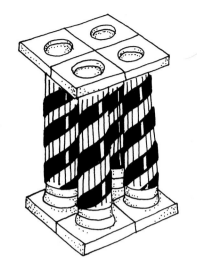

Figure 1

tops of the columns to hold them together (figure 1).

To make the hat, carve out a square at the bottom of the Styrofoam cone the same size as the top of the columns, so that the hat will fit over them at an angle, as shown in the photograph. Cover the hat with beige fondant, then make a brim with another piece of fondant measuring $2\frac{1}{2}$ inches wide by the circumference of the base of the cone. Dampen the back of this strip and attach it to the bottom of the cone, allowing the top of the brim to curve away from the hat. Place pieces of paper towel between the hat and the brim to hold the brim in place as it dries (figure 2).

Hot-glue the hat to the top of the columns. With the #17 tip, pipe blue royal icing in a circular motion over the bottom of the hat. Use the #68 tip to attach the ribbons, loops, bird, flowers on stems, and leaves with green royal icing. Add a fabric rose to the center of the bow.

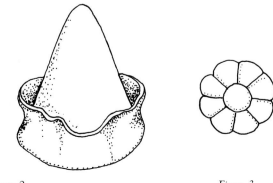

Figure 2   *Figure 3*

Make 32 gum-paste buttons from the center of the medallion in the Wilton Baroque mold kit (figure 3). Let dry. Brush with gold paint.

To decorate the cake:

Bake the cakes and let them cool completely. Assemble the tiers on their corresponding foamcore boards. Cut a slice from the bottom tier measuring 6 inches wide and 2 inches deep, and cut a corresponding slice from the foamcore board. Make sure that the slice is only 2 inches deep, because it shouldn't extend under the 14-inch tier that will be above it. Crumb-coat the inside of the slice (page 146).

Cover the 8-, 14-, and 18-inch tiers with white rolled fondant. Quilt the 14-inch tier immediately, using a flexible cardboard triangle for the sides of the cake (see page 171).

Tint some fondant royal blue and cover the petal-shaped tier. Insert the dowels in each tier.

Place the 18-inch tier on the prepared base. Use the #127 tip to pipe a white ruffle of royal icing around the bottom edge of the cake. Then pipe 2 more ruffles, slightly overlapping, above the first one. Using the #2 tip and pale-blue royal icing, pipe a small zigzag along the edge of the bottom ruffle. Let dry.

Mix yellow iridescent powder with lemon extract and paint the quilted tier. Use royal icing to attach large silver dragées to the intersections of the quilt lines.

For the 8-inch tier, pipe the floral pattern as shown on pages 98 and 99, using white royal icing and the #2 tip. Let dry. Dust the design with pink powdered coloring.

To make the draped skirt on the 18-inch tier, mark around the tier 4 inches from the bottom with a toothpick. Roll out some fondant $\frac{1}{8}$ inch thick and cut it into a 15-by-3-inch strip. Brush the back, just at the top, with a little water. Attach it to the cake at the mark, gently folding and ruffling the strip as you attach it. Prop up the bottom with crumpled paper towels until it dries. Repeat, rolling and adding fondant strips until the skirt is complete. Fold the edge of each strip under the edge of the previous one.

To make the puffy top of the skirt, work in sections again, propping up the fondant with marshmallows to keep its shape. Knead the marshmallows until

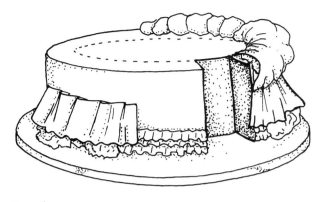

Figure 4

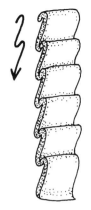

Figure 5

they are slightly sticky and attach them to the top edge of the tier. Cut a 15-by-4-inch strip of fondant. Brush the top and bottom edges with a little water. Attach the strip, slightly folded, to the top of the cake, just where the 14-inch tier will start. Place the strip over the marshmallow edge, creating an even seam. Smooth the seam and cut it if necessary (the seam will be hidden by a ribbon). Hide the ends of each strip under the previous one, as you did for the skirt (figure 4).

When the skirt is complete, use the 1-inch cutter to make circles of fondant. Brush them with a little water and attach them randomly around the skirt. Use royal icing to attach the red ribbon around the seam. Brush the bottom edge of the skirt with gold paint.

Stack the tiers. On the blue tier, use the #45 tip to pipe pink vertical buttercream ruffles at the separation between each scallop (figure 5). Pipe the same ruffle around the base of the 8-inch tier. Then pipe a snail trail of blue icing on both sides of the ruffle, using the #2 tip. Place 4 gold buttons vertically on each scallop,

as shown in the photograph. Attach a medium dragée in the center of each button with a dot of royal icing. Use the #20 tip to pipe blue buttercream shells around the bottom edge.

To make the rope border for the quilted tier, roll out 2 long ropes of fondant, $\frac{1}{2}$ inch wide and the length of the circumference of the cake. Twist them together and wrap them around the base of the tier. Brush with yellow iridescent paint.

Attach the 5 bows and ribbons evenly around the bottom tier, using green royal icing. Place a rose in the center of each and pipe royal-icing leaves around them with the #66 tip.

Attach the royal-icing roses and the apple gum-paste blossoms to the cut-out area on the bottom tier, using green royal icing and the #66 leaf tip.

Attach the hat ornament to top of the cake with royal icing. Use the #68 tip and white royal icing to pipe leaves around the base of the columns.

Sweet Hearts

I designed this lavish cake for *Modern Bride* magazine as variations on a theme. Each tier is decorated to resemble the top ornament, a sugar mold of an antique quilted candy box. A variety of pastel flowers made of gum paste complete the romantic vision.

Serves 148

Cakes:
    9-inch heart, 3 inches high
    12-inch heart, 4 inches high
    15-inch heart, $4\frac{1}{2}$ inches high
6-inch heart pan
rolled fondant (page 142)
ruler
gum paste (page 155)
nontoxic white iridescent and gold powder
lemon extract
small paintbrush
gold dragées
royal icing (page 144)
wax paper
gum-paste decorations (pages 155–166):
    50 small and 50 medium pink roses
    25 pink petunias, 5 of them on stems
    40 bunches of 10 lavender tiny blossoms
       and buds

55 small, medium, and large pale-green
    leaves, 15 of them on stems
60 small white buds
5-inch Styrofoam heart, $1\frac{1}{2}$ inches high
moss-green paste food coloring
22-inch heart-shaped base, $\frac{1}{2}$ inch thick
white glue
$\frac{1}{2}$-inch-wide white ribbon to cover the edge of
    the base
9-, 12-, and 15-inch heart-shaped foamcore
    boards
flexible cardboard
right triangle
X-acto knife
tracing wheel
$\frac{1}{4}$-inch-thick wooden dowels
pastry bags and couplers
tips #2, #66, and #68

In advance:

Make the 2 sugar molds in the 6-inch heart pan, one 2 inches deep for the box bottom, and the other, 1 inch deep, for the lid. Hollow each mold before it dries completely. When the molds are dry, cover the shorter one with rolled fondant and quilt it (see page 171). Cover the sides of the other mold with rolled fondant.

    Make 2 gum-paste loops and 2 ribbons about $\frac{1}{2}$ inch wide for the top of the box. Place a $\frac{1}{2}$-inch-wide diagonal gum-paste ribbon on top of the quilted box (figure 1). When the gum-paste decorations are dry, mix white iridescent powder with a little lemon extract and paint them. Attach gold dragées along all of the

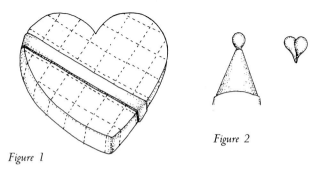

Figure 1

Figure 2

edges, using white royal icing piped from the #2 tip.

    Make 200 small hearts in royal icing on wax paper (figure 2). Let dry. Brush them with gold paint made

by combining gold powder and lemon extract. Let dry. Attach some to the corners of the quilted squares on the sugar mold, using dots of royal icing.

Make all of the gum-paste flowers, buds, and leaves. Let dry.

Attach the Styrofoam heart to the center of the deeper sugar mold with royal icing. Tint some royal icing moss-green. Start placing the flowers, buds, and leaves on stems in the heart, using the #68 tip to pipe green icing around the base of each stem. Prop the lid on the box where it will be attached to help you position the flowers. Use the #66 tip to pipe pale-green royal-icing leaves around the edge of the box to finish.

Trace an outline of the largest cake pan on the base as described in the section on making bases (page 173). Cover the base with thinned royal icing. Let dry. Glue the ribbon along the edge of the base.

To decorate the cake:

Bake the cakes and let them cool completely. Assemble the tiers on their corresponding heart-shaped boards. Cover one tier at a time with rolled fondant and quilt immediately, before it dries. Cut a flexible cardboard triangle with the X-acto knife for quilting the sides of the cake.

Insert dowels in the 2 largest tiers. Place the bottom of the sugar box on the top tier and position the lid, marking the fondant with a toothpick where you want to place the box and the lid. Remove the molds and insert dowels at the marks.

Using dots of royal icing piped from the #2 tip, attach small gold royal-icing hearts to all of the tiers at the intersections of the quilted lines. Handle the hearts with tweezers to prevent the gold from coming off on your hand.

Stack the tiers on the prepared base. Attach the flowers and leaves around the bottoms of all the tiers, using green royal icing and the #66 tip. Pipe leaves in the spaces between the flowers.

Attach the box to the top of the cake with royal icing. Pipe a dot border of white royal icing around the bottom, using the #2 tip. Angle the lid on the box as shown in the photograph and attach it with royal icing. Glue the loops and ribbons in the center of the lid, using green royal icing piped from the #66 tip. Add a few small flowers and royal icing leaves.

Birch-Bark Cake

The idea for a rustic-looking wedding cake came to me after I saw some dried flower arrangements that resembled cakes. If dried flowers can be arranged to look like a cake, I thought, why not make a cake to look like a lovely array of dried flowers?

Serves 150

Cakes:
  12-inch round, 4 inches high
  16-inch round, $4\frac{1}{2}$ inches high
royal icing (page 144)
royal-icing decorations (pages 150–154):
  18 medium and 23 large purple Canterbury
    bells
  40 burgundy chrysanthemums
  25 small lavender roses
  11 large pink roses
  45 small and 70 medium pink rosebuds
  325 baby's breath, in clusters of 3
  1 blue and 1 monarch butterfly made of
    run-in sugar (page 170)
wax paper
black and green powdered food coloring
lemon extract
small paintbrush
paper towels
4 black stamens

10 #20 cloth-covered wires 12 inches long
white florist's tape
black marking pen
20-inch round base, $\frac{1}{2}$ inch thick
white glue
$\frac{1}{2}$-inch-wide white ribbon to cover the edge of
  the base
white modeling chocolate (page 141)
12- and 16-inch round foamcore boards
basic buttercream icing (page 139)
pasta machine or rolling pin
pizza cutter
$\frac{1}{4}$-inch-thick wooden dowels
orange, brown, blue, moss-, leaf-, and
  kelly-green paste food coloring
small and large pointed leaf cutters
pastry bags and couplers
tips #16, #68, and #70

In advance:

Make all of the royal-icing decorations (for the butterfly wings, use patterns 1 and 2). Let dry. Paint both sides of the butterfly wings with black, blue, and orange coloring mixed with lemon extract, as shown in the patterns and in the photograph. When the wings are dry, tint a small amount of royal icing black and use the #16 tip to pipe a line of icing about $1\frac{1}{2}$ inches long on a piece of wax paper. Place 2 wings in the icing and use crumpled paper towels to prop them up at an angle to dry. Insert 2 black stamens in the wet icing for antennae. Let the butterflies dry completely.

Make the birch branch for the top of the cake out

of 10 12-inch-long wires. Start wrapping one end of the bunch of wires with white florist's tape. Continue taping as you separate the wires into branches extending from the trunk. Cut the branches into different lengths and tape them as well (figure 1). With a marking pen, draw black horizontal lines on the tape to resemble birch bark (figure 2).

Cover the base with thinned white royal icing. Let dry. Glue ribbon around the edge.

Make the modeling chocolate and let it rest overnight.

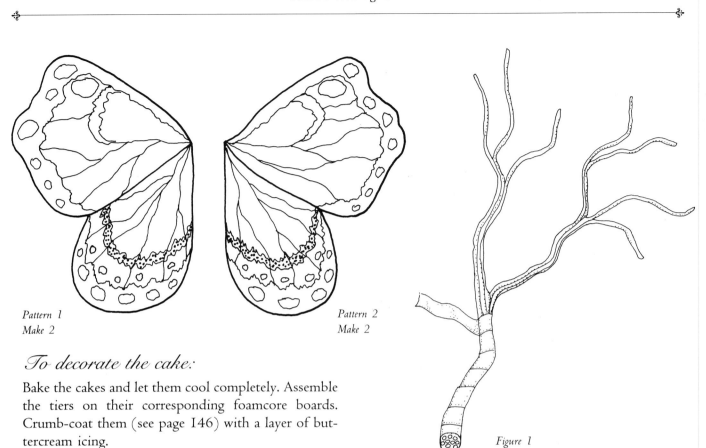

Pattern 1
Make 2

Pattern 2
Make 2

Figure 1

To decorate the cake:

Bake the cakes and let them cool completely. Assemble the tiers on their corresponding foamcore boards. Crumb-coat them (see page 146) with a layer of buttercream icing.

To cover the sides of each tier with strips of white modeling chocolate, first roll the chocolate through a pasta machine to get an even thickness. You can also use a rolling pin, but the pasta machine is easier. Lightly dust the work surface with a little confectioners' sugar to keep the chocolate from sticking. Run the chocolate through the machine several times, starting at the widest setting, until the chocolate is about $\frac{3}{16}$ inch thick. Use a pizza cutter to cut the strips to the exact height of each tier. Press them to the sides of the cakes.

Insert dowels in the bottom tier and stack the tiers on the prepared base.

To create the birch-bark effect on the chocolate, score long and short horizontal slashes with the tip of a sharp knife. Mix black powdered coloring with lemon extract and paint the marks.

Tint some of the modeling chocolate with powdered green coloring and cut out 11 small and 46 large leaves with the pointed cutters. Press the large leaves at an angle onto the bottom sides of the tiers, using the photograph as a guide. Curve the small leaves slightly and set them aside.

Position the flowers in concentric circles on the cake, using green buttercream piped from the #68 and #70 leaf tips to hold them in place. Place 12 medium rosebuds in a circle around the top center. Arrange the remaining flowers, using the photograph as a guide. Place the 11 small chocolate leaves upright between the Canterbury bells and the roses on the top tier.

Place the branch on top of the cake and pipe a little green royal icing to hold it in position.

Attach the butterflies to the cake and the branch with a little royal icing, as shown in the photograph.

Figure 2

Chocolate Groom's Cake

The tradition of the groom's cake dates from the mid-nineteenth century, when guests took home slices of a dark fruitcake that was not served at the wedding. Those who were unmarried would slip their slices under their pillow to encourage dreams about their future mate. Although this tradition has faded, it's still fun to serve a dark chocolate cake along with the white "bride's cake."

Serves 20

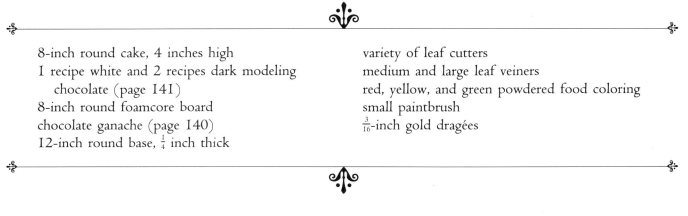

8-inch round cake, 4 inches high
I recipe white and 2 recipes dark modeling
  chocolate (page 141)
8-inch round foamcore board
chocolate ganache (page 140)
12-inch round base, $\frac{1}{4}$ inch thick

variety of leaf cutters
medium and large leaf veiners
red, yellow, and green powdered food coloring
small paintbrush
$\frac{3}{16}$-inch gold dragées

In advance:

Make the modeling chocolate and let it sit overnight.

To decorate the cake:

Bake the cake and let it cool completely. Place it on the 8-inch foamcore board. Fill and cover the cake with a smooth layer of chocolate ganache. Place the cake on the 12-inch base.

Take a little modeling chocolate of each type and knead together slightly until they are just marbled. On a surface lightly dusted with confectioners' sugar, roll the chocolate about $\frac{1}{16}$ inch thick. Cut out various leaves and cover the base around the cake with them.

Roll out some dark chocolate and cut large leaves using pattern 1. The leaves should be about $\frac{1}{8}$ inch thick. Vein them with the large leaf veiner and attach them to the sides of the cake at a slight angle. The pointed top of the leaf should extend about $\frac{1}{2}$ inch over the top of the cake. Cover the sides of the cake, overlapping the leaves a bit (figure 1).

Knead some green coloring into the white chocolate. Cut out and vein enough rose leaves to cover the bottom edge of the cake.

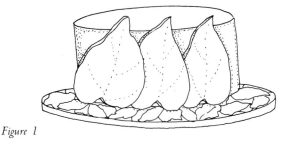

Figure 1

To make the fruit and gourds, roll white modeling chocolate into $\frac{3}{8}$-inch balls for 2 bunches of grapes, then shape 3 1-inch apples, 3 1-inch oranges, 3 1$\frac{1}{2}$-inch-long pears, and 3 1$\frac{1}{2}$-inch-long gourds. Brush them with the appropriate powdered coloring and attach them to the cake. Make a few green leaves for the top of the grape bunches and sprinkle a few dragées on the cake.

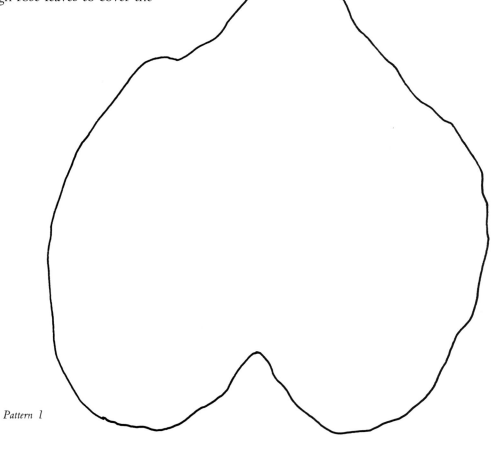

Pattern 1

Love in Bloom

I designed this cake out of a desire to come up with an unusual shape that could be made without special pans. It turned out to be simple: I cut square cakes in half diagonally and stacked the triangles so that they were stepped in front and level in back to form a cake with a different look on each side.

Serves 135

Cakes:
  6-inch square, $1\frac{1}{2}$ inches high
  8-inch square, $1\frac{1}{2}$ inches high
  10-inch square, $1\frac{1}{2}$ inches high
  12-inch square, $1\frac{1}{2}$ inches high
  14-inch square, $1\frac{1}{2}$ inches high
gum-paste flowers (pages 155–166):
  30 peach-colored tulips
  75 pink sweet peas
  65 purple bellflowers
  130 small purple blossoms made with the
    apple-blossom cutter
  30 white dogwood blossoms
4 yards of gold sheer wire-edged ribbon, $2\frac{1}{4}$
  inches wide
royal icing (page 144)
pastry bags and couplers
tips #1.5, #2, and #352
nontoxic gold and white iridescent powder
lemon extract

small paintbrush
11 white #20 cloth-covered wires, 10 inches
  long
wax paper
6-, 8-, 10-, 12-, and 14-inch foamcore squares,
  cut in half diagonally to form triangles
X-acto knife
18-inch foamcore square, $\frac{1}{2}$ inch thick, cut in
  half diagonally
$21\frac{1}{2}$-inch foamcore square, $\frac{1}{2}$ inch thick, cut in
  half diagonally
white glue
$\frac{1}{2}$-inch-wide white or gold ribbon to cover the
  edges of the bases
rolled fondant (page 142)
$\frac{1}{4}$-inch-thick wooden dowels
5 white #26 cloth-covered wires, 6 inches long
green paste food coloring
basic buttercream icing (page 139)

In advance:

Make all of the gum-paste flowers and let them dry.

To decorate the ribbons, cut 4 lengths 21 inches long and one length 60 inches long. Spread them out flat. Thin about 2 tablespoons of royal icing slightly, so that a piped dot ends without a point. Using figure

1, pipe the design on the ribbon with the #2 tip. Let dry for a few hours. Paint the dots with gold powder mixed with lemon extract.

Bend the 10-inch wires into spirals and leaves (figures 2–4). On a flat surface covered with wax paper,

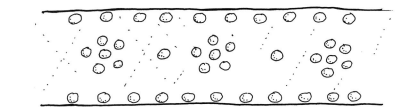

Figure 1

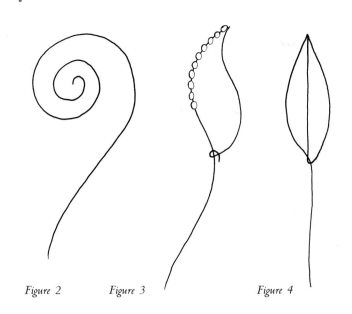

Figure 2   Figure 3   Figure 4

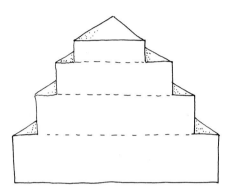

with the longest edges flush so that the back of the cake forms a flat surface. The front of the cake is stepped (figure 6).

Make the bow for the top of the cake by folding the ribbon into 5 equal loops. Tie the loops together with a piece of 6-inch white wire. Insert the wire in the top of the cake. Twist a wire around one end of each of the other ribbons. Cut a notch in the end of each ribbon.

Figure 6

use the #1.5 tip to pipe white royal-icing dots along the length of the wires, leaving about 2 inches exposed at the end. Let dry, then pipe dots on the other side and let dry. Paint the dots with white iridescent powder mixed with lemon extract.

Cut the triangle foamcore bases. Glue the 18-inch board on top of the 21½-inch one, placing heavy books on top to keep them flat while the glue dries. Cover the boards with thinned white royal icing. Glue the ribbon to the edge of the bases.

To decorate the cake:

Bake the cakes and let them cool completely. Cut all of the cakes in half diagonally (figure 5) and assemble them on their corresponding foamcore boards. Cover with rolled fondant. Insert the dowels. Stack the tiers

Tint some royal icing pale green and begin placing the flowers in the cake, using the photograph as a guide. Start to insert 45 purple bellflowers down the front of the cake. Use the #352 tip to pipe buttercream leaves between the flowers.

Place a ribbon down the length of the cake on each side of the flowers, inserting the wired end into the top of the cake, under the bow. Arrange the ribbons and pipe a little royal icing to hold them in place. Place 23 tulips next to the ribbon on the right side of the cake and 15 dogwood blossoms on the left, attaching the dogwoods with royal icing. Pipe leaves among the flowers.

Add ribbons to the cake alternately with flowers, inserting 37 sweet peas on the left and 60 small purple blossoms on the right. Insert the wired pearl shapes, using the photograph as a guide.

Insert the remaining flowers in the back of the cake, piping leaves between them.

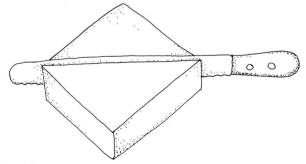

Figure 5

Chapeau des Fleurs

This wedding cake was featured in a display by the hat designer Lola at Bergdorf Goodman in New York City. I used the design of one of Lola's hats for the top, then placed it on a cake stand inside another cake that is an all-white version of Lola's striped hatbox.

Serves 250

2 16-inch round cakes, 3 inches high

18-inch round base, $\frac{1}{2}$ inch thick

royal icing (page 144)

$\frac{1}{2}$-inch-wide white ribbon to cover the edge of the base

white glue

gum paste (page 155)

gum-paste decorations (pages 155–166):

    3 large white roses, $3\frac{1}{2}$ inches wide

    3 medium white roses

    7 large white leaves

    6 white loops, 2 to 3 inches long

    4 white ribbons, 2 of them 5 inches long and 2 of them 12 inches long

nontoxic white iridescent powder

lemon extract

small paintbrush

50 royal-icing baby's breath (page 154)

8-inch-wide Styrofoam cylinder, 6 inches high

14-inch-wide Styrofoam disk, $1\frac{1}{2}$ inches high

rolled fondant (page 142)

16-inch-high clear plastic cake stand with a 9-inch-wide plate (found in cake-decorating supply stores)

tape measure

ridged rolling pin

pizza cutter

ruler

green florist's tape

2 16-inch round foamcore boards

$\frac{1}{4}$-inch-thick wooden dowels

scalloped edge crimper

flexible cardboard

30-60-90-degree triangle

X-acto knife

tracing wheel

pure white royal buttercream icing (page 139)

pastry bags and couplers

tips #3, #8, and #10

In advance:

Cover the base with thinned royal icing. Let dry. Glue the ribbon around the edge of the base.

Make the gum-paste roses, leaves, and loops. Next, make the long ribbons and let them dry in gentle curves (figure 1). Make sure that they are *completely* dry before placing them on the hat. When they are dry, mix white iridescent powder with lemon extract and paint the outside of the loops and *one side* of the ribbons (if you paint the back of the ribbon, it will not adhere to the cake). Paint three leaves and brush the ends of the rose petals with the paint. Make the royal-icing baby's breath.

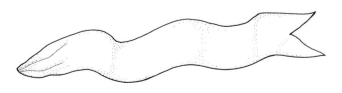

Figure 1

To make the brim of the hat, trace the outline of the 8-inch Styrofoam cylinder in the center of the 14-inch disk with a marking pen. Sand the 14-inch disk with another piece of Styrofoam to shape the brim so that it faces down in the front and curves up

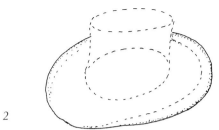

Figure 2

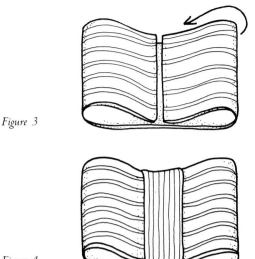

Figure 3

Figure 4

in the back (figure 2). Turn the brim upside down and roll out a piece of fondant big enough to cover the bottom of the brim, reach over the edge, and extend around the other side to the 8-inch circle. Before placing the fondant on the bottom of the brim, brush it with a little water to make it adhere to the sides and top. Smooth the fondant over the edge, then turn the brim over and smooth the top. Cut the fondant at the 8-inch circular mark. Let it dry overnight.

Next, cover the 8-inch Styrofoam cylinder with fondant. Attach the hat to the brim, inside the 8-inch mark, with royal icing. Glue the bottom of the hat to the plate of the cake stand.

To decorate the hat, first measure the circumference of the 8-inch cylinder with a tape measure. Roll out a piece of fondant to this length and at least 3 inches wide. Roll the fondant about $\frac{1}{4}$ inch thick, then carefully roll it once with the ridged rolling pin, parallel to the length of the strip, keeping the ridges straight. Straighten and trim the edges with the pizza cutter. Turn the strip over and brush it with water. Attach it to the bottom edge of the hat, placing the seam in the back (the brim edge that curls up).

To make the ribbon, cut a 10-inch-long strip of fondant, 3 inches wide, and roll it with the ridged rolling pin, as above. Brush the ends of the back of the strip with water. Fold the ends to meet in the center of the strip (figure 3). Place some crumpled paper towels inside the loops to keep them from collapsing while you make the center piece. Cut another strip measuring $3\frac{1}{2}$ by 2 inches. Wet the back and place it on the center of the bow, tucking in the ends at the top and bottom (figure 4). Stand the bow up, wet the back, and attach it to the hat band at the seam.

Brush the band and bow with white iridescent paint. Gather groupings of 5, 7, or 10 baby's breath and tape them together with green florist's tape. Use royal icing

to attach the 3 large roses to the brim on the front of the hat. Attach loops around the roses. Attach the ribbons to the brim, placing the shortest one on the left front and the other three on the right side, with the longest two facing up and away from the hat. Finally, attach the leaves and baby's breath around the hat, using the photograph as a guide.

To make the gum-paste tissue paper that covers the top of the cake, you will need about 4 pounds of gum paste. Roll out sheets of paste as thin as possible. Cut into triangles and rectangles with the pizza cutter and fold to look like crumpled paper. Dry the pieces on a paper-towel-covered cookie sheet, propping up some sections with extra paper (figure 5). Let dry overnight.

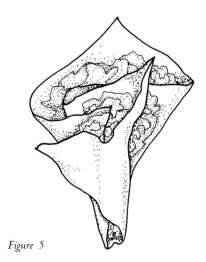

Figure 5

To decorate the cake:

Bake the cakes and let them cool completely. Place a 3-inch-high filled layer of cake on a 16-inch foamcore board and crumb-coat it (page 146). Roll out some fondant and cut out a 16-inch circle. Place the fondant on the cake layer. Insert the dowels, then place the other 3-inch filled and crumb-coated layer on its 16-inch board on top. Cover the entire cake with rolled fondant. Crimp the top edge.

Cut a flexible cardboard triangle with the X-acto knife. Quilt the sides of the cake (see page 171) with 2 diagonal lines $1\frac{1}{2}$ inches apart, then 3 lines $\frac{1}{2}$ inch apart, repeating this pattern around the cake (figure 6). Paint every other stripe with white iridescent paint. Using the #3 tip, pipe a snail trail along the 2 quilted lines on each side of the $\frac{1}{2}$-inch painted lines.

Insert the cake stand in the center of the cake. Pipe

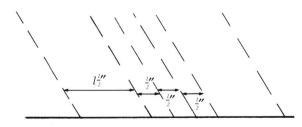

Figure 6

a thick border of royal icing around the base of the stand to hold it in place. (*Note:* Do not deliver the cake with the hat on the stand; add the hat when it reaches its final destination.) Pipe a buttercream dot border with the #10 tip around the bottom edge of the cake. Pipe the hat box handle, using the #8 tip and the rope technique.

Place the gum-paste tissue paper on top of the cake, holding it in place with dots of royal icing.

Oriental Apple Blossoms

At this spring wedding, the table settings inspired the theme for the cake. The decorations echo the Oriental floral motif and blue border of the china patterns, and the centerpieces of apple blossoms and roses.

Serves 225

Cakes:

6-inch round, 3 inches high

10-inch round, 3 inches high

14-inch round, 3 inches high

18-inch round, $3\frac{1}{2}$ inches high

3 sugar molds (page 170):

a cup $3\frac{1}{2}$ inches wide at the top, $1\frac{3}{4}$ inches wide at the base, and $2\frac{1}{2}$ inches high

a circle cutter $1\frac{3}{4}$ inches wide and 1 inch high

a tart pan 3 inches wide at the top, $1\frac{3}{4}$ inches wide at the base, and 1 inch high

royal icing (page 144)

3-inch-wide Styrofoam egg

wax paper

gum-paste decorations (pages 155–166):

40 pale-pink apple-blossom branches with buds

40 large white roses

20 small white roses and buds

30 tiny blossoms

40 pale-yellow lotus flowers, 20 of them on stems

75 large and small green leaves

$\frac{1}{2}$-inch-wide white ribbon to cover the edge of the base and wrap around the columns

4 columns, 5 inches high

7 columns, 7 inches high

hot-glue gun

2 7-inch and 2 11-inch separator plates

4-inch Styrofoam ball, cut in half

moss-green paste food coloring

24-inch round base, $\frac{1}{2}$ inch thick

white glue

14- and 18-inch round foamcore boards

rolled fondant (page 142)

$\frac{1}{4}$-inch-thick wooden dowels

tape measure

18-inch metal ruler

pizza cutter

diamond-shaped crimpers

lilac cutter

trumpet-flower tool

nontoxic gold and blue iridescent powder

lemon extract

small paintbrush

pastry bags and couplers

tips #2, #13, and #16

In advance:

Make the sugar molds. Hollow only the cup. Let dry. Attach the circular mold to the smaller end of the tart mold with a little royal icing. Then attach the stand to the cup. Let dry. Attach the Styrofoam egg, wide end up, in the hollow of the vase, using royal icing.

To pipe the royal-icing design on the vase, place the vase on a piece of wax paper, holding it in place with a dab of icing. Use the #13 tip to pipe vertical lines around the circular mold, then use the #16 tip to pipe shells above and below the lines. Pipe another set of shells above the top shells. Around the top edge of the vase, pipe a double row of shells. Pipe #16 shells around the base, then overpipe with #13 shells (figure 1). Let the icing dry before you add the flowers, because the design also reinforces the seams between the molds.

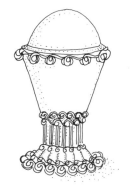

Figure 1

Make the gum-paste flowers and leaves.

When the flowers are dry, wrap white ribbon around the columns, securing it with hot glue at the top and bottom. As you wind the ribbon, wrap an apple-blossom branch tightly against each column. Place the 5-inch columns on the pegs on one of the 7-inch separator plates, with the blossoms facing outward. Place 4 of the 7-inch columns on the pegs on the 11-inch plate and hot-glue the 3 remaining columns between them on 3 sides of the plate.

Using royal icing, attach a Styrofoam half-ball to the center of each bottom separator plate. Make the flower arrangements on the half-balls and in the sugar vase, holding them in place with moss-green royal icing piped with the #16 tip.

Cover the base with thinned royal icing. Let dry. Glue white ribbon around the edge of the base.

To decorate the cake:

Bake the cakes and let them cool completely. Assemble the tiers on their corresponding foamcore boards or separator plates. Cover with rolled fondant and insert dowels in all of the tiers, including the top. Stack the 18- and 14-inch tiers on the prepared base.

To make the embossed borders of rolled fondant, measure the circumference of each tier with the tape measure. Working on one tier at a time, cut strips of fondant 1 inch wide, $\frac{3}{16}$ inch thick, and the circumference of the tier, using the metal ruler and the pizza cutter. (For the large tier, you may have to make 2 strips and piece them together.) Dampen the back of a fondant strip with water to make it tacky, then press the strip onto the edge of its tier. With the crimpers, emboss diamonds $\frac{1}{4}$ inch apart all around the strip.

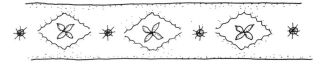

Figure 2

Press the lilac cutter into the center of each diamond, then press the trumpet-flower tool between the diamonds (figure 2).

When all of the borders are embossed, mix the powdered coloring with lemon extract and paint the diamonds blue and the embossed stars gold. Paint the top edge of the borders gold.

Stack the remaining tiers and columned separator plates. Attach the flowers and leaves with royal icing, as shown in the photograph.

Summer

Summertime Fantasy

An eighteenth-century English woven porcelain basket adorned with realistic ceramic flowers and berries gave me the idea for this latticework cake and its luxuriant blooms.

Serves 250

Cakes:
   $6\frac{1}{2}$-by-9-inch rectangle, $4\frac{1}{2}$ inches high, made
      in a 9-inch square pan
   $10\frac{1}{2}$-by-13-inch rectangle, 4 inches high,
      made in an 11-by-15-inch pan.
   13-by-16-inch rectangle, 4 inches high,
      made in 2 9-by-13-inch pans
   16-by-20-inch rectangle, $4\frac{1}{2}$ inches high,
      made in an 18-by-24-inch pan
gum-paste decorations (pages 155–166):
   3 white and 5 yellow freesia branches
   7 purple and 16 blue morning glories
   6 blue half-open morning glories
   12 morning-glory buds
   80 small and medium stephanotis
   10 red poppies
   10 pale-pink tulips with red stripes
   4 roses and 18 rosebuds
   12 large petunias
   13 mimosa branches
   20 primulas
   100 leaves
   150 pink tiny blossoms with yellow-dot
      centers
   11 raspberry branches

4 sugar molds (page 170):
   2 made in a cup, $2\frac{1}{2}$ inches high and
      $3\frac{1}{4}$ inches wide
   2 made in a tart pan, 1 inch high and
      $2\frac{1}{2}$ inches wide
royal icing (page 144)
2 Styrofoam balls, 3 inches wide
wax paper
oval block of Styrofoam, 6 inches long by
   $4\frac{1}{4}$ inches wide and 3 inches high
rolled fondant (page 142)
pink and moss-green paste food coloring
5 foamcore rectangles, 23 by 30 inches and
   $\frac{1}{4}$ inch thick
X-acto knife
ruler
white glue
$\frac{1}{2}$-inch-wide white ribbon to cover the edge of
   the base
4 foamcore rectangles corresponding to the
   sizes of each tier
pure white royal buttercream icing (page 139)
$\frac{1}{4}$-inch-thick wooden dowels
pastry bags and couplers
tips #2, #4, #5, #6, #17, #20, #48, and #67

In advance:

Make all of the gum-paste decorations. Let dry.

Make the sugar molds. Hollow out the 2 cups, leaving the tart molds solid. Let dry. To make the vases, attach the bottom of a cup mold to the bottom of a tart mold with a little royal icing. Let dry. Place a Styrofoam ball in each vase, using royal icing to secure it. Set the vases on a piece of wax paper with a little royal icing to hold them in place. Use the #17 tip to pipe a white royal-icing shell border around the

seam joining the 2 molds on each vase. Pipe vertical lines of icing in the grooves on the base with the #5 tip. Pipe another shell border around the bottom edge of the base. Let dry.

The royal-icing lattice panels must be piped very carefully so they will fit each side of the cake. Make a template for each panel size, following the chart below. Place each template on a cookie sheet and cover it with wax paper. Pipe white diagonal lines in a criss-

Figure 1

cross pattern, using the #48 ribbon tip and following the pattern lines shown in figure 1. Using the #5 tip, pipe diagonal lines between the first lines (figure 1). (*Hint:* To make the panels exactly the correct size, pipe the icing slightly past the line on the pattern. Then, while the icing is still wet, use a palette knife to cut off the excess icing at the line on the pattern. This will give you a clean and precise edge for each panel.) Let dry.

MEASUREMENTS FOR LATTICEWORK PANELS

For the top tier:	$4\frac{1}{4} \times 1\frac{1}{2}$ inches	(make 4)
	$4\frac{1}{4} \times 3\frac{1}{2}$ "	(make 2)
	$4\frac{1}{4} \times 5\frac{1}{2}$ "	(make 2)
For the second tier:	$3\frac{3}{4} \times 2\frac{1}{2}$ inches	(make 4)
	$3\frac{3}{4} \times 5\frac{1}{2}$ "	(make 2)
	$3\frac{3}{4} \times 7\frac{1}{2}$ "	(make 2)
For the third tier:	$3\frac{3}{4} \times 4$ inches	(make 4)
	$3\frac{3}{4} \times 6\frac{1}{2}$ "	(make 2)
	$3\frac{3}{4} \times 8\frac{1}{2}$ "	(make 2)
For the bottom tier:	$4\frac{1}{4} \times 5\frac{3}{4}$ inches	(make 4)
	$4\frac{1}{4} \times 7\frac{1}{2}$ "	(make 2)
	$4\frac{1}{4} \times 9\frac{1}{2}$ "	(make 2)

To make the basket for the top of the cake, sand the 3-inch-high block of Styrofoam smooth until it measures $5\frac{3}{4}$ by $4\frac{1}{4}$ inches (see pattern 1). Cover it with green rolled fondant. Do the piping with the basket set upside down, so the top of the basket will be larger than the bottom. Tape the oval pattern on a flat sur-

face and cover it with a sheet of wax paper. Attach the Styrofoam, uncovered side down, to the center of the oval, using a dab of royal icing. With the #6 tip, pipe strings of white royal icing diagonally from the top down to the edge of the outer oval. Pipe all of the lines marked on the oval in one direction, then in the other connecting the top mark to the lower marks to its left and right. The lines will be curved (see figure 2). Overpipe the lines in the same order with the #4 tip. Pipe a scalloped border with the #6 tip around the outer edge of the lines on the wax paper. Let dry for at least 24 hours.

When the basket is dry, carefully remove it from the wax paper by turning it over and pulling the paper away from the icing. Place it upright on another piece of wax paper and pipe another scalloped border over the first one at the top. Let it set for a few minutes, then overpipe another. Pipe a shell border at the bottom, using the #20 tip. Let dry.

Insert the stemmed flowers, leaves, and berries into the top of the basket and the sugar vases. Use the #67 tip to pipe green royal icing at the base of each flower to hold it in place. Attach loose leaves around the outer edge.

Cut the boards for the stepped cake base from the 5 foamcore rectangles with an X-acto knife, using the dimensions given in figure 3. The middle board should be one board thick, while the top and bottom boards should each be 2 boards thick. Glue the boards together and place heavy books on top to keep them flat while the glue dries. Cover the tops of the boards with a layer of thinned pink royal icing. Let dry. Using

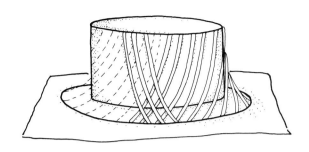

Figure 2

the #5 tip, pipe a white royal-icing dot border around the edge of the middle board. Glue ribbon around the edge of the top and bottom boards.

To decorate the cake:

Bake the cakes and let them cool completely. Cut the foamcore boards for each tier, using the dimensions given in figure 4. Assemble the tiers on a flat surface. Center the corresponding board on top of each tier. With a serrated knife, cut the tiers vertically, using the boards as a template. Place a dab of royal buttercream icing on each cake and attach the boards, then invert the cakes and boards. Cover the cakes with pink buttercream icing. Insert the dowels and stack the tiers on the prepared base.

Attach the lattice panels to the sides of the tiers with buttercream icing, using the #17 tip. Attach tiny blossoms at every other intersection on the lattice panels, using dots of royal icing. Pipe white buttercream shell borders around the base and top edge of each tier. Pipe zigzag borders of buttercream at the intersections of each of the panels, using the #20 tip.

Place the finished basket on top and attach the rest of the flowers and leaves to the cake with dots of royal icing, using the photograph as a guide. Place the 2 sugar vases on each end of the base and attach them with royal icing.

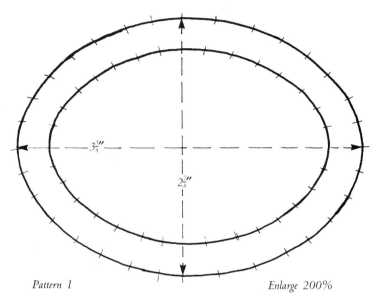

Pattern 1 $3\frac{5}{8}''$ $2\frac{7}{8}''$ *Enlarge 200%*

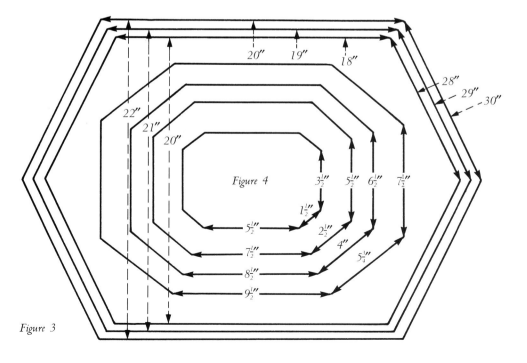

Figure 3 *Figure 4*

Coral Reef

For a summer wedding by the sea, why not decorate a cake with starfish, seashells, and coral? Although they look as real as any you'd find on the beach, they're completely edible. The coral color of the cake itself adds whimsy and originality to the occasion.

Serves 60

Cakes:
 $7\frac{3}{4}$-by-$5\frac{5}{8}$-inch oval, 4 inches high
 13-by-$9\frac{7}{8}$-inch oval, 5 inches high
gum paste (page 155)
small and large plastic seashell molds (available at candy or cake-decorating stores)
seashells and dried starfish (optional)
cornstarch
nontoxic white iridescent powder
lemon extract
small paintbrush
royal icing (page 144)
wax paper
cookie sheet

brown, red, and black powdered food coloring
pink, blue, purple, and yellow paste food coloring
19-by-15-inch oval base, $\frac{1}{2}$ inch thick
$\frac{1}{2}$-inch-wide white or coral-colored ribbon to cover the edge of the base
white glue
2 oval foamcore boards, the same sizes as the cake pans
basic buttercream icing (page 139)
$\frac{1}{4}$-inch-thick wooden dowels
pastry bags and couplers
tips #1, #2, #3, #5, and #20

In advance:

There are several ways to make the 15 gum-paste starfish and 45 shells of various sizes needed for this cake; all are equally easy. You can use ready-made chocolate molds for the seashells, but they come in a limited number of shapes and sizes. To create your own molds out of gum paste, use real shells and dried starfish that you have collected. Make sure they are clean and dry before you begin.

To make a mold, shape a piece of soft gum paste as wide and a little deeper than the object you want to mold. Press the object, top side down, into the paste until it is level with the top. Carefully remove the object without disturbing the imprint and dust the inside of the mold with cornstarch. Allow the mold to dry for a few days or longer, if possible, to help ensure that it won't break or crack.

When you are ready to make the decorations, take a piece of soft gum paste about the same size as the cavity of the gum-paste or chocolate mold and dust it with cornstarch to keep it from sticking. Press it into the mold, making sure to fill the cavity completely. You can also make a hollow shell by pressing in a thin sheet of gum paste. Carefully remove the paste and let it dry on a paper towel dusted with cornstarch.

Make a few pearls by rolling gum paste into small balls about $\frac{1}{4}$ inch in diameter. When they are dry, paint them with white iridescent powder mixed with lemon extract.

You can also make piped shells out of stiff white royal icing. Place wax paper on a cookie sheet. Using the #5 tip, pipe a 2-by-$\frac{1}{2}$-inch cone in a circular motion (figure 1).

To make sand dollars, place a piece of wax paper on a cookie sheet. Using royal icing and the #2 tip, pipe the outline of a small circle and a larger circle the size of each of the patterns provided (patterns 1 and 2). Make about 5 of each size. Thin about 1 cup of royal icing with a little water, a few drops at a time,

Figure 1

until a teaspoonful of icing dropped into the cup disappears by the count of 15. Fill in the patterns with the thinned royal icing and let them dry for at least 24 hours. Use the #1 tip to pipe small dots of royal icing, as indicated on the patterns.

To make coral, use royal icing and the #3 and #5 tips. Place a piece of wax paper on a cookie sheet and coat it very lightly with shortening. Pipe lines in a treelike shape, using pattern 3 as a guide and alternating tips as needed. Let the lines overlap to give the coral added strength and dimension. Let dry for 24 hours. Before lifting from the paper, carefully dust some of the pieces with red or brown powdered food coloring, using a soft paintbrush.

Color the dried shells and starfish with powdered or liquid colors, using real shells as a guide. For a mother-of-pearl effect, paint the inside of the shell with thinned blue and purple coloring, then cover it lightly with the white iridescent paint.

Finally, make the run-in sugar shells that form the collars around the top of the tiers (see page 170). Place a piece of wax paper on a cookie sheet. Using patterns 4 and 5, pipe the outlines with white royal icing with the #2 tip. Fill in with thinned royal icing. Let dry for at least 24 hours.

To make the shell border for the base, transfer pattern 6 to the base with a pencil, then outline and fill in the shells, as above. Tint about 2 cups of royal icing coral by combining pink and yellow coloring. Thin the icing to run-in consistency. Using the #2 tip, fill in the areas around the shells and the entire base. Let dry. Glue ribbon around the edge of the base.

To decorate the cake:

Bake the cakes and let them cool completely. Assemble the tiers on their corresponding foamcore boards. Tint some buttercream icing coral to match the base. Buttercream tends to darken as it dries, so make it a shade lighter than the royal icing. Cover the cakes with buttercream icing. Insert the dowels and stack the tiers on the prepared base. Pipe a buttercream rope border around the bottom of each tier, using the #20 star tip.

Place the shells, starfish, sand dollars, and coral around the cake as shown in the photograph, using dots of royal icing to hold them in place.

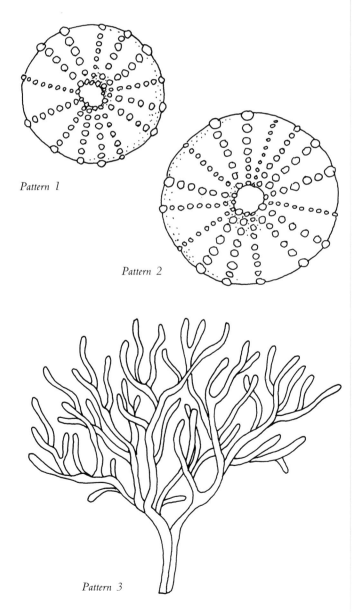

Pattern 1

Pattern 2

Pattern 3

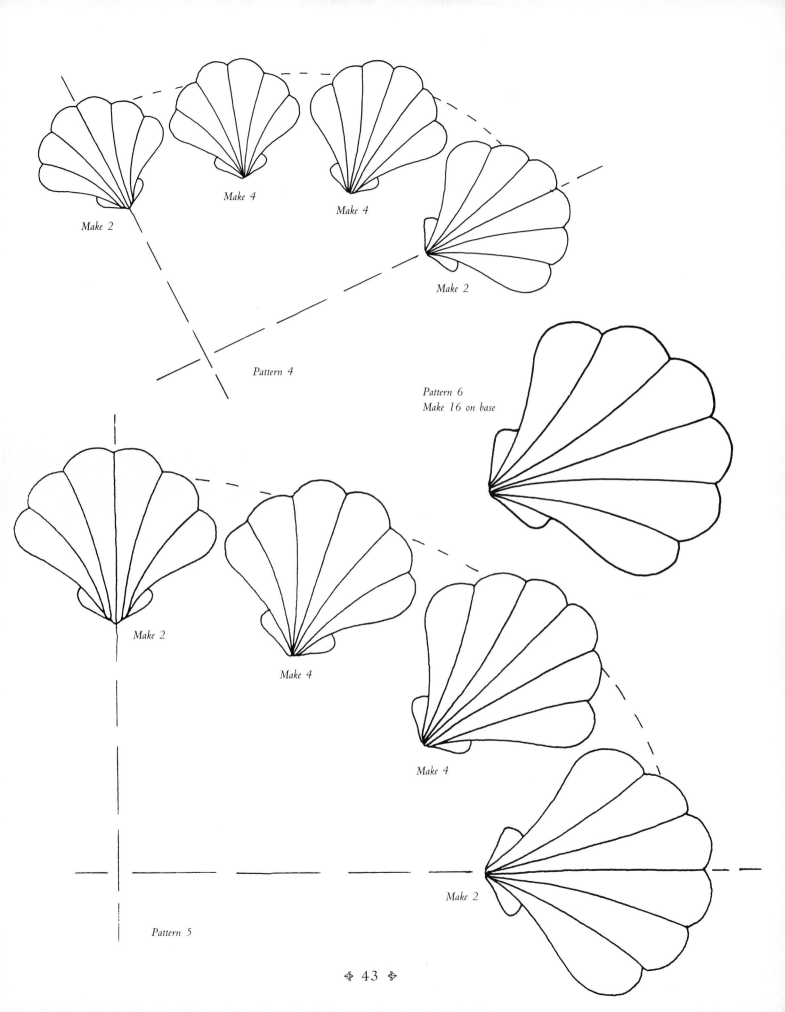

Make 2

Make 4

Make 4

Make 2

Pattern 4

Pattern 6
Make 16 on base

Make 2

Make 4

Make 4

Make 2

Pattern 5

Enchanted Garden

Perfect for a summer wedding, this charming cake is festooned with rows of colorful royal-icing flowers and crowned by a lush bouquet.

Serves 85

Cakes:
  6-inch round, 3 inches high
  8-inch round, 3 inches high
  12-inch round, 3 inches high
  royal-icing flowers (pages 150–154):
    12 blue morning glories, 5 of them on stems
    10 blue morning-glory buds
    10 marigolds, 5 of them on stems
    15 red multi-petaled daisies with yellow centers, 7 of them on stems
    8 yellow asters with red centers, 4 of them on stems
    44 large and small pale purple Canterbury bells, dusted with red, 22 of them on stems
    8 yellow-orange anemones, 4 of them on stems
    8 orange chrysanthemums with red centers, 4 of them on stems
    7 coral azaleas, 3 of them on stems
    18 medium white roses and 17 rosebuds,

dusted with pink, 17 of them on stems
    6 white lilies, dusted with coral, 3 of them on stems
    10 pink petunias, 5 of them on stems
    20 lavender and 20 white baby's breath
    15 lavender and 15 yellow 5-petal daisies, 15 of them on stems
    20 coiled wires
royal icing (page 144)
15-inch round base, $\frac{1}{2}$ inch thick
moss-green, eggshell, and yellow paste food coloring
$\frac{1}{2}$-inch-wide yellow ribbon to cover the edge of the base
white glue
3-inch-wide Styrofoam ball, cut in half
6-, 8-, and 12-inch round foamcore boards
basic buttercream icing (page 139)
$\frac{1}{4}$-inch-thick wooden dowels
pastry bags and couplers
tips #22, #80, and #352

In advance:

Make all of the royal-icing flowers. Let dry.

Cover the base with thinned eggshell-colored royal icing. Glue the ribbon around the edge of the base.

To make the bouquet for the top of the cake, insert the stemmed royal-icing flowers into the Styrofoam half-ball and hold them in place with green royal icing piped from the #22 tip.

To decorate the cake:

Bake the cakes and let them cool completely. Place each cake on its corresponding foamcore board. Fill and cover the cakes with pale-yellow buttercream, the same shade as the icing on the base. Insert the dowels

Figure 1

and stack the cakes on the prepared base.

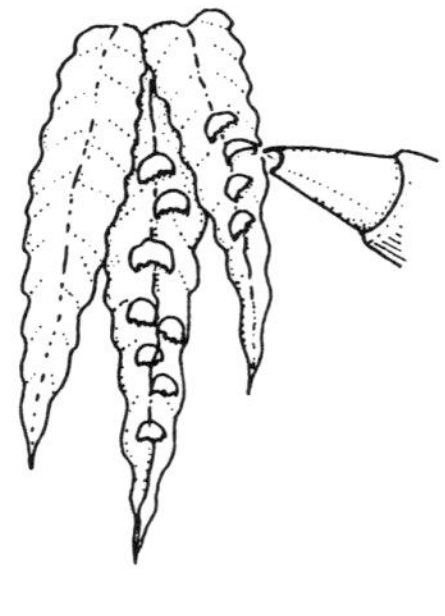

Using pale-yellow buttercream and the #22 tip, pipe shell borders around the bottom edge of all of the tiers.

Pipe lilies-of-the-valley on each tier before you add the royal-icing flowers. Using pale-green buttercream

and the #352 tip, pipe leaves of varying lengths down the sides, using the photograph as a guide. Then pipe the lily-of-the-valley flowers over the leaves with white buttercream and the #80 tip. Hold the tip so that the end resembles an upside-down U, then position it perpendicular to and touching the cake. Apply steady pressure, letting the icing build up slightly, then pull the tip away and down, relaxing pressure as you break

off the end. Each flower should resemble a little half-cup (figure 1).

To add the royal-icing flowers, use the #352 tip to pipe green buttercream leaves and attach flowers on them. Place the flowers randomly on the leaves, using the photograph as a guide. After the flowers are in place, fill in any empty spaces with leaves.

Dotted-Swiss Cake

Puffs of dotted flocked tulle add a touch of lightness and intriguing contrast to this cake. When the bride and groom, Janis Koffler and David Adler, walked in as we were photographing the cake at the Lotos Club in New York City, they were happy to pose for us.

Serves 175

Cakes:
    8-inch round, 4 inches high
    12-inch round, 4 inches high
    16-inch round, 4 inches high
1 roll 4-inch-wide dotted flocked tulle
    (available from Offray Ribbon)
#26 white cloth-covered wires
royal-icing decorations (pages 150–154):
    20 large white lilies, 5 of them on stems
    20 medium coral azaleas, 4 of them on
        stems
    20 small yellow chrysanthemums, 7 of them
        on stems
    30 pink-edged daisies, 10 of them on stems
    15 small and 15 medium pink roses, 6 of
        them on stems
    30 purple bachelor's buttons, 10 of them on
        stems
    30 purple hyacinths

75 baby's breath
25 green leaves on stems
3-inch-wide Styrofoam ball, cut in half
royal icing (page 144)
2 9-inch separator plates
4 5-inch columns
green paste food coloring
pastry bags and couplers
tips #1, #2, #18, and #68
aluminum foil
20-inch round base, $\frac{1}{2}$ inch thick
$\frac{1}{2}$-inch-wide white ribbon to cover the edge of
    the base
white glue
12- and 16-inch round foamcore boards
rolled fondant (page 142)
$\frac{1}{4}$-inch-thick wooden dowels
basic buttercream icing (page 139)

In advance:

Make 18 tulle bows. Cut a length of tulle about 18 inches long. Make 2 loops in the center and let the ends extend in equal lengths. Tie in the center with a 6-inch white wire to secure (figures 1 and 2).

    Make all of the royal-icing decorations and let them dry. Attach a Styrofoam half-ball to the center of one 9-inch separator plate with royal icing. Make sure that the pegs on the plates are facing up. Place the columns on the pegs and insert the stemmed royal-icing flowers and leaves in the Styrofoam, piping green royal icing with the #18 tip around the base of each stem.

    Cover the bottom of the other half-ball with foil. Add a tulle bow to the top, then insert stemmed flowers and leaves into the ball.

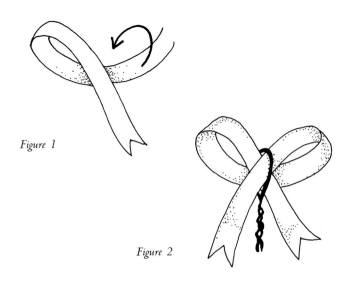

Figure 1

Figure 2

Cover the base with thinned royal icing. Glue ribbon around the edge of the base.

To decorate the cake:

Bake the cakes and let them cool completely. Assemble the 2 larger tiers on their corresponding foamcore boards and the top tier on the second separator plate. Cover all three tiers with white fondant. Insert the dowels and stack the tiers, separator plates, and columns on the prepared base.

Following the patterns on pages 98 and 99, pipe a brocade design on all the tiers in white royal icing. Use the #1 tip for the small dots and the #2 tip for the rest of the design.

Insert the wired bows evenly around the cake, 6 on each of the lower tiers and 5 on the top tier. Arrange flowers between the bows. Pipe green buttercream leaves with the #68 tip to hold the flowers in place. Place the bouquet on top, securing it with a little royal icing. Add flowers without stems on the cake around the bottom of the ball.

Sugar Shack

A little house with a white picket fence — is there a more traditional American dream for young newlyweds? The charming country cottage on top can be saved as a memento.

Serves 100

Cakes:
  9-inch square, 3 inches high
  12-inch square, $3\frac{1}{2}$ inches high
  16-inch square base, $\frac{1}{2}$ inch thick
  royal icing (page 144)
  $\frac{1}{2}$-inch-wide white ribbon to cover the edge of
    the base
  white glue
  wax paper
  large piece of foamcore
  X-acto knife
  metal ruler
  piping gel
  leaf-, kelly-, and moss-green, black,
    golden-yellow, and purple paste food
    coloring
  2 9-inch foamcore squares
  3 ice-cream cones for the trees
  white cotton balls
  white royal-icing decorations (pages 150–154):

480 daisy petals, made with the #104 tip
288 daisy petals, made with the #102 tip
44 rosebuds
48 $\frac{3}{4}$-inch-long loops, made with the
  #102 tip
12 $\frac{1}{2}$-inch-long ribbons, made with the
  #102 tip
12 2-inch-long ribbons, made with the
  #102 tip
cookie sheet
purple powdered food coloring
small paintbrush
12-inch foamcore square
pure white royal buttercream icing (page 139)
$\frac{1}{4}$-inch-thick wooden dowels
pastry bags and couplers
tips #1, #2, #3, #16, #18, #21, #46, #48,
  #52, #65S, #65, #70, #102, #104, #233,
  #1D, and #2B

In advance:

Cover the base with white royal icing and glue ribbon around the edge.

Pipe the picket-fence pieces for the sides and top of the cake in royal icing on wax paper, following patterns 1–5. Use the #48 tip for the top fence and the #2B and #1D tips for the fences on the tiers. Let dry.

Cut out foamcore pieces for the house, using patterns 6–11. With the X-acto knife, bevel the side edges of all of the pieces for the house and chimney, as well as the top edges of the roof pieces (figure 1). The bevel should slant toward the back of each piece. Cut out the door on the front and save it. Spread

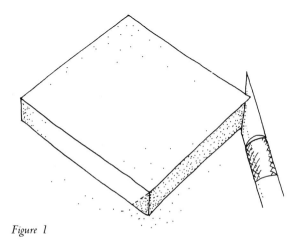

Figure 1

lavender-tinted piping gel in the window areas, as indicated on the pattern.

To decorate the house pieces, pipe horizontal lines of white royal icing with the #2 tip, then fill in with run-in sugar (see page 170). Let dry. The roof will be decorated after it is placed on the house.

Pipe the chimney bricks on patterns 9–11 with the #46 tip. After piping each horizontal row, use a toothpick to make divisions between the bricks. Let the pieces dry. Assemble the chimney, using royal icing piped inside the corners to hold the 4 pieces together. Let dry.

Following figure 2, draw the outline for the base of the house and fence in the center of one of the 9-inch foamcore squares. Draw the front walk. Assemble the house on the square, piping royal icing to hold it together on the base. Let the house dry. Join the roof pieces at the beveled edges and attach them to the house with royal icing.

To decorate the roof, use the #102 tip to pipe a row of scallops in royal icing along the bottom edge, letting them overhang slightly. Repeat, piping each row so that it slightly overlaps the row below, until the roof is covered, as shown in pattern 8. Place the chimney in the wet icing on the roof. Using the #2 tip, pipe outlines around the scallops and a zigzag border along

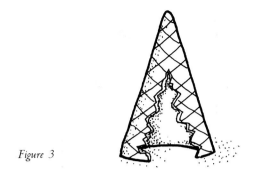

Figure 3

the top and sides of the chimney and the edges of the roof. Pipe dots in the center of each scallop. Pipe a shell border on top, using the #18 tip.

To make the trees, break off pieces of the ice-cream cones (figure 3) so that they will fit on the board at the corners of the house, as indicated in figure 2. Attach the cones to the board with white royal icing. Tint some royal icing with kelly and moss green. Starting at the bottom of each cone, pipe branches with the #18 tip, pulling the icing out to a point until the cone is completely covered. Pipe thick green spirals for the bushes around the base of the house, using the #21 tip.

Tuck a little cotton in the chimney to simulate smoke.

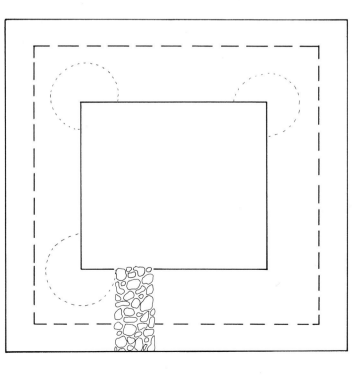

Figure 2

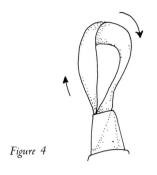

Figure 4

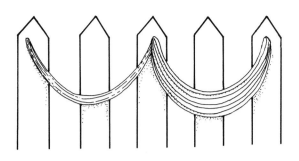

Figure 5

Tint some royal icing with leaf and kelly green. Using the #233 tip, pipe grass around the house up to the line for the fence. Place the smallest fence pieces upright in the wet icing, joining them at the corners. Finish piping the grass on the rest of the board.

Pipe the flowers and vines on the fence with the #1 tip, as shown in the photograph. Use pale-green royal icing for the stems, yellow dots for the centers of the flowers, white dots for petals, and small purple rosettes for roses. Pipe tiny green leaves with the #65S tip.

Make all the royal-icing decorations. To make the loops, fit the #102 tip onto a pastry bag. Place a sheet of wax paper on a cookie sheet. Hold the tip perpendicular to the paper, with the wide end facing down. Keeping the tip upright, pipe a loop (figure 4), making sure that it ends with a point. Let dry.

Brush the ends of the rose petals with a little purple powdered coloring.

To decorate the cake:

Bake the cakes and let them cool completely. Assemble the tiers on their corresponding foamcore boards. Cover them with 2 layers of white buttercream icing. Insert the dowels and stack the tiers on the prepared base.

Assemble the fence on the sides of each tier, using a little royal icing to hold the pieces in place. Pipe royal-icing strings between the fences with the #16 tip. Use the #3 tip to pipe 6 smaller strings over the #16 string (figure 5).

Pipe a buttercream shell border around the bottom of each tier, using the #21 tip. Pipe a small rosette of buttercream icing with the #18 tip for the center of each large daisy, at the center of the 2 strings. Place large daisy petals in the rosette with the wide ends facing out from the center of the flower. Tint some

royal icing yellow and pipe over the center with the #233 tip.

Tint some buttercream moss green and pipe leaves around each daisy with the #70 tip. Place a rosebud on each side of the daisies in the green icing. Pipe some smaller leaves around the buds with the #65 tip. Tint some buttercream pale purple and pipe lilacs around the other flowers with the #52 tip. Use the #16 tip to attach the smaller daisies in the centers of the strings with a small rosette of white royal icing. Attach the petals and pipe the yellow centers. Pipe small green royal-icing leaves on both sides.

Place the house on top of the cake. Pipe a white royal-icing shell border around the edge of the grass area, using the #18 tip.

Finish the cake by attaching the ribbons and loops to the tops of the strings with white royal icing, using the photograph as a guide.

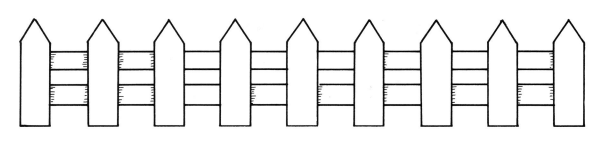

Pattern 1
Make 3

Enlarge Patterns 130%

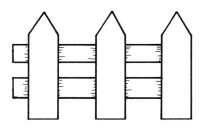

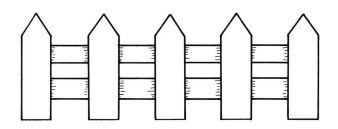

Pattern 2
Make 1

Pattern 3
Make 1

Pattern 4
Make 4

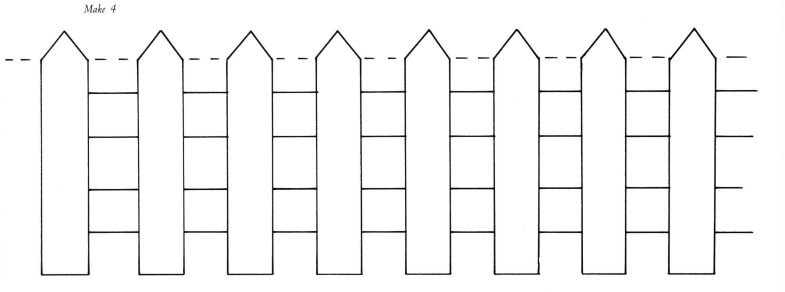

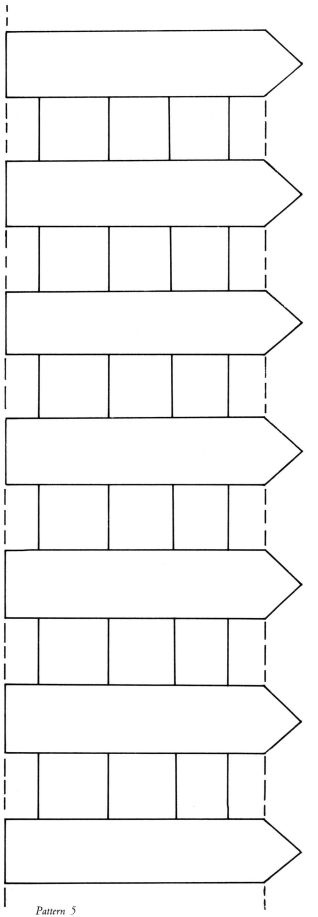

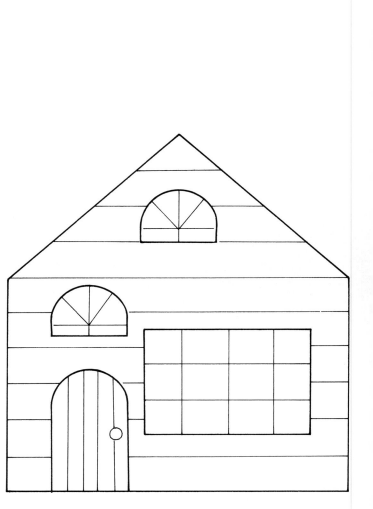

Pattern 6
Front and Back of House, Make 2

Pattern 5
Make 4

Enlarge Patterns 130%

Pattern 7
Sides of House, Make 2

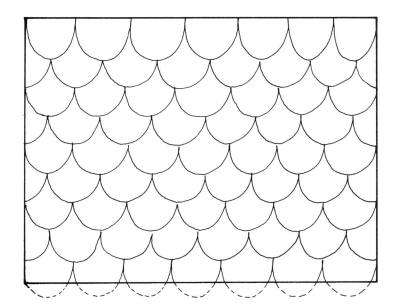

Pattern 8
Roof, Make 2

Pattern 9
Chimney, Make 2

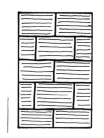

Pattern 10
Chimney, Make 1

Pattern 11
Chimney, Make 1

Strawberry Cake

What could be more fitting for a June wedding than a cake adorned with fresh strawberries? But don't let your eyes deceive you — these berries are fashioned with modeling chocolate. The decorations are rolled-fondant cutouts. Even the ants are made of royal icing! Although real ants are often unavoidable at summer outings, these wedding guests are strictly optional.

Serves 175

Cakes:
 8-inch round, 3 inches high
 12-inch round, 3 inches high
 16-inch round, 3 inches high
2 sugar molds (page 170):
 I, made in a cup $3\frac{1}{2}$ inches wide and
  $2\frac{1}{2}$ inches high
 I, made in a tart pan $3\frac{1}{2}$ inches wide and
  $\frac{3}{4}$ inch high
rolled fondant (page 142)
royal icing (page 144)
small paintbrush
white modeling chocolate
grater
toothpicks
Styrofoam for drying strawberries
red and green powdered food coloring
lemon extract

I eggwhite or meringue powder
small rolling pin
small daisy cutter
calyx cutter
20-inch round base, $\frac{1}{2}$ inch thick
$\frac{1}{2}$-inch-wide white ribbon to cover the edge of
 the base
white glue
8-, 12-, and 16-inch round foamcore boards
$\frac{1}{4}$-inch-thick wooden dowels
small sharp knife
large leaf veiner
5 leaf cutters
2 primula cutters
brown paste food coloring
pastry bags and couplers
tips #0, #2, and #3

In advance:

To make the sugar vase and stand from the molds, hollow out the cup mold, but leave the tart-pan mold solid. When both are dry, cover them with rolled fondant. Attach the stand to the vase with a little royal icing. Let dry. Roll out two 12-inch ropes of fondant about $\frac{1}{4}$ inch thick. Brush with a little water and wrap one around the separation between the vase and the stand, and the other around the outer edge of the base, as shown in the photograph.

Make the modeling chocolate and let it set overnight, wrapped in plastic. To form the strawberries, roll the chocolate into 50 large and small strawberry shapes. Roll each strawberry on the smallest holes of a grater to add texture. Place the wide end of each strawberry on the end of a toothpick and place the toothpick in a piece of Styrofoam. Mix some red powdered coloring with a little lemon extract and paint the strawberries, holding them by the toothpick. When the color is dry, paint each strawberry with lightly beaten eggwhite or a mixture of I tablespoon of meringue powder dissolved in 2 tablespoons of hot water. Brush lightly to avoid causing the red color to come off.

Knead a 2-inch ball of modeling chocolate in a little powdered green coloring. Roll out the chocolate as thin as possible on a surface dusted with a little confectioners' sugar. Cut out the calyxes (the green top of the strawberry) with the small daisy cutter (for the small strawberries) and the calyx cutter (for the larger ones). Roll each petal to elongate it, remove the toothpick from the strawberry, and press the calyx onto the berry.

Cover the base with thinned white royal icing and let dry. Glue the ribbon around the edge.

To decorate the cake:

Bake the cakes and let them cool completely. Place the layers on their corresponding foamcore boards and crumb-coat them (see page 146). Cover with fondant. Insert the dowels and stack the tiers on the prepared base.

Roll out some fondant to about $\frac{1}{8}$ inch thick. Use pattern 1 to cut out large leaves with a sharp knife. Press each leaf onto a large leaf veiner, brush the back with a little water, and attach it to the cake. Cover the cake with large leaves, using the photograph as a guide. Cut out smaller leaves, using the various leaf cutters. Attach the medium-sized leaves, then the small ones.

Cut out large and small fondant flowers with the primula cutters and attach them to the cake in the spaces between the leaves. Shape pieces of fondant into strawberry halves with flat bottoms. Roll them on the grater for texture. Brush the flat side with water and attach the half-berries to the cake. Cover the vase and stand with leaves and flowers.

Using white royal icing and the #2 and #3 tips, pipe stems and clusters of berries around the cake (figure 1). Attach the vase to the top of the cake with a little royal icing. Fill it with chocolate strawberries. Place the remaining strawberries around the cake, fixing them in position with dots of royal icing.

To make the ants, use the #0 tip to pipe a ¼-inch line of brown royal icing. Pipe 3 perpendicular lines on each side of the line for the legs. Then pipe a dot on both ends of the center line to finish.

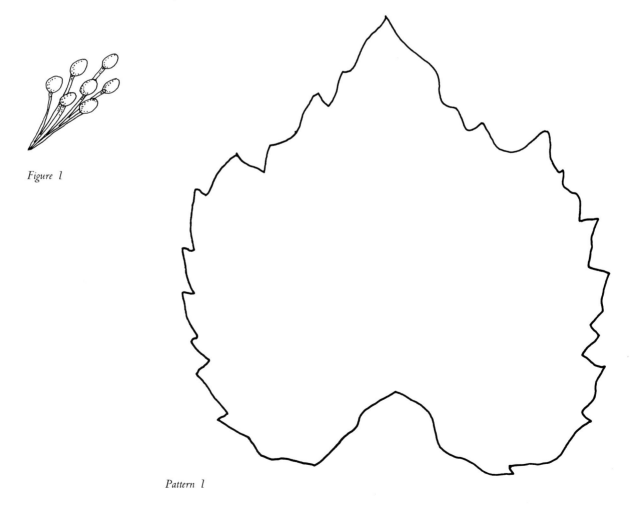

Figure 1

Pattern 1

Independence Day Wedding Cake

I designed this cake for *Modern Bride* magazine to depict the spirit of Victorian patriotism, with bunting swags and a festooned gazebo. It's perfect for a summertime wedding near the Fourth of July, or for any wedding with a red, white, and blue theme.

Serves 450

Cakes:
  $7\frac{3}{4}$-by-$5\frac{5}{8}$-inch oval, 3 inches high
  2 8-inch round, 4 inches high
  2 12-inch round, 4 inches high
  2 16-inch round, 6 inches high
gum paste (page 155)
small wooden rolling pin
toothpicks
royal icing (page 144)
wax paper
small paintbrush
red and blue paste food coloring
$\frac{7}{8}$- and $1\frac{1}{4}$-inch-wide star cutters
nontoxic gold powder
lemon extract
X-acto knife
22-inch foamcore square

metal ruler
white glue
roll of $2\frac{1}{2}$-inch-thick masking tape
$\frac{1}{4}$-inch-thick wooden dowels
water-based white paint
4 foamcore rectangles, one 8 by 15 inches, one 12 by 17 inches, and two 16 by 27 inches
3 foamcore rectangles, 23 by 34 inches each
$\frac{3}{4}$-inch-wide white ribbon to cover the edge of the base
foamcore oval, same size as oval cake pan
rolled fondant (page 142)
pizza cutter
tape measure
pastry bags and couplers
tips #2, #3, #14, #18, and #45

In advance:

Cut out a small 1-by-2-inch triangle of gum paste and dampen the straight edge opposite the point. Wrap the end around a round toothpick and let the triangle dry in a wavy position. This will be the flag for the top of the gazebo.

Make the 7 run-in sugar railings (see page 170), using pattern 1.

Make 8 small gum-paste bunting swags for the top of the gazebo and 3 large swags for the cake. To make each small swag, cut a strip of gum paste 1 inch wide and 6½ inches long. Fold it accordion-style (figure 1), then hold the gathers at the center with one hand and spread the other side into a half-circle (figure 2). Place

Pattern 1
Railing, Make 7

on a paper towel to dry completely. For the 3 larger swags, use strips that measure 3 by 12, 3 by 15, and 4 by 20 inches. Let these dry on paper towels in a V shape about 1 inch deep so they will fit into the contour of the cake.

Make 10 ruffled gum-paste buttons between 2 and 4 inches wide. One button has 1 ruffle, 2 buttons have

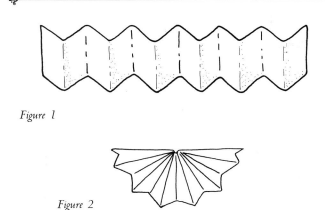

Figure 1

Figure 2

2 ruffles, and one has 3. To make a ruffle, cut a strip of gum paste 1 to $1\frac{1}{2}$ inches wide, depending on the size of the finished button. Fold into pleats (figure 3), forming a circle, and brush one end with water to stick the ends together. Let dry completely. Make gumpaste disks, 2 red and 2 blue, each about 1 inch wide.

When the garlands and buttons are dry, use the #2 tip to pipe red and blue royal-icing stripes on the edges, as shown in the photograph. Let dry. To assemble the buttons, pipe some white royal icing in the center of the largest ruffle and place a smaller ruffle on top, alternating red and blue borders. Add a third smaller ruffle if necessary, then attach the center button, also alternating red and blue.

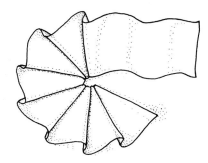

Figure 3

Cut out 26 gum-paste stars, using the star cutters (you will need 8 small stars for the gazebo). Let these dry, then paint them with gold powder mixed with lemon extract.

To make the gazebo, cut out 3 foamcore octagons made from 6-inch circles, 2 made from $5\frac{1}{2}$-inch circles, and 3 made from $5\frac{1}{4}$-inch circles, all cut from the 22-inch foamcore square (see page 173). Glue the 3 6-inch octagons together with white glue, then glue one of the $5\frac{1}{2}$-inch octagons on top. Next, glue 2 of the $5\frac{1}{4}$-inch octagons on top of the other 4.

To make the roof, cut 8 foamcore triangles, using pattern 2. Bevel all 3 sides of each triangle with the X-acto knife. Glue the triangles on top of the remaining $5\frac{1}{2}$-inch octagon so that they meet at a point in the center. Hold them in place with masking tape while the glue dries. Glue the remaining $5\frac{1}{4}$-inch octagon on the underside of the roof. When the roof is dry, remove the tape and cover the top with smooth white royal icing.

Pattern 2
Roof, Make 8

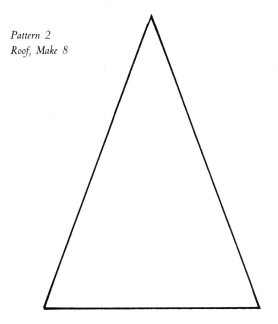

Cut 8 dowels, each 3 inches long. On the small octagon on the base, mark 8 circles $\frac{1}{4}$ inch wide $\frac{1}{4}$ inch in from each corner. Glue the dowels at these marks, making sure that they are perfectly straight (figure 4). Let dry. Paint the dowels white and let them dry. Glue the roof on top of the dowels, evenly centered. Let dry.

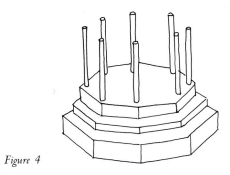

Figure 4

Pipe a little white royal icing around the base of each dowel to secure them.

Place the gazebo on a piece of wax paper with a dab of royal icing. Attach a small gum-paste ball to the point on top with a little water and insert the flag. Use the #3 tip to pipe a dot border of white royal icing along the edges of all of the triangles. Using the #18 tip, pipe a zigzag border of royal icing along all the cut edges on the base of the gazebo. With a little royal icing, attach the small swags to the top edge of the roof. Pipe a shell border along the tops of the swags, using the #14 tip. Attach the 8 small stars to the corners of the roof.

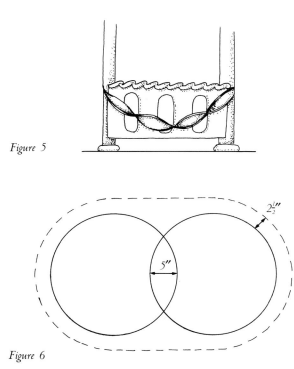

Figure 5

Figure 6

boards for the 2 16-inch tiers). Place one of the boards on a 23-by-34-inch piece of foamcore and outline with a $2\frac{1}{2}$-inch-thick roll of tape (see figure 6 and page 173). Cut 3 of these ovals and glue them together, weighing them down with heavy books to keep them flat while the glue dries. Cover with thinned white royal icing. Let dry. Glue ribbon around the edge of the base.

To make the boards for the tiers, outline the bottoms of the oval, the 8-, and the 12-inch cake pans on their corresponding foamcore rectangles, overlapping them as shown in figure 7.

Figure 7

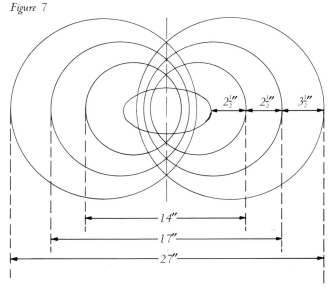

Place the 7 run-in sugar railings between the dowels, slightly above the floor, and attach them with royal icing.

Roll out and cut strips of red gum paste measuring $1\frac{3}{4}$ by $\frac{1}{4}$ inch. Twist them and attach the ends to the dowels around the top of the railings with a little water (figure 5). Let the gazebo dry completely.

To make the oval base for the cake, use the 16-inch cake pans to outline 2 circles on one of the 16-by-27-inch foamcore rectangles, overlapping the circles by 5 inches (figure 6). Repeat (these will also serve as the

To decorate the cake:

Bake the cakes and let them cool completely. Add the filling and cut the cakes to match the outlines of the foamcore boards. Assemble the tiers on the boards, holding the cut edges together with icing. The 16-inch tier should be constructed as 2 tiers, with a board and dowels on top of the first 3-inch layers. Cover the top with a layer of fondant before placing the second board. Crumb-coat each cake (see page 146), then cover it with a thin layer of rolled fondant. Insert the dowels.

The cakes should be decorated starting at the bottom, with the next tier then being stacked and decorated, and so on. Cut a 6-by-12-inch strip of rolled fondant with the pizza cutter and slice it at a diagonal on each side. Dampen the back and attach it to the front of the bottom tier, ruffling the bottom as you

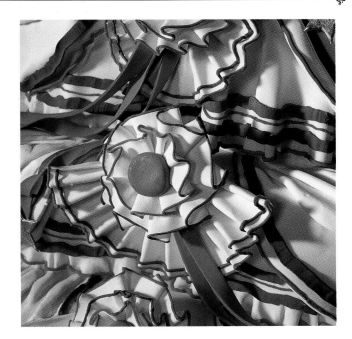

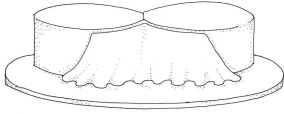

Figure 8

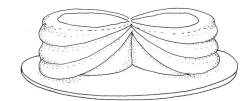

Figure 9

attach it (figure 8). Measure from the front top of the cake down around and up to the top of the back, using a tape measure. Cut a 4-inch-wide strip of fondant to that measurement. Dampen the back of the top edge and attach it to the cake, folding it slightly as you do. Repeat on the other side of the cake. Cut another strip the same size and attach it above the first, hiding the bottom by rolling it under the first strip. Repeat on the other side and continue until the bottom tier is covered. The pieces should all meet at one point in the back (figure 9).

Add the next tier and cover it in the same manner as the bottom tier. Add the third tier and decorate to match. Decorate the fourth tier so that the fondant drapes off-center, as shown in the photograph.

Make some red and blue royal icing. Using the #45

tip, pipe 2 blue stripes horizontally across the front ruffle of all of the tiers. Pipe another blue stripe parallel to the edge of the draping around the cake. Use the #3 tip to pipe red stripes along the edges and between the blue lines on the front ruffles.

Attach pleated bunting to the front of each tier with royal icing. Prop it up with toothpicks while the icing dries.

Cut red gum-paste strips $\frac{3}{8}$ inch wide to hang down from the tops of the bunting swags. Attach them to the cake with a little water, using the photograph as a guide. When the bunting is dry, attach the ruffled buttons to the top center with royal icing. Attach the gold stars to the ends of the gum-paste ribbons with small dots of royal icing. Secure the gazebo on top with a little royal icing.

Majolica Cake

Majolica is a type of pottery that originated in the 1850s and is now very popular with collectors. These lustrous glazed ceramics typically depict butterflies, fruits and vegetables, flowers, and fans in bold colors and charming designs — the perfect inspiration for a festive, brightly colored cake!

Serves 110

Cakes:
- 6-inch round, 3 inches high
- 9-inch hexagon, 5 inches high
- 14-inch round, 5 inches high
- 2 sugar molds (page 170):
  - 1, made in a cup 2 inches high and 4 inches wide
  - 1, made in a bell 3 inches high
- royal icing (page 144)
- 3-inch-wide Styrofoam ball
- rose-petal, yellow, purple, moss-green, royal- and sky-blue, brown, red, and orange paste food coloring
- gum paste (page 155)
- leaf cutters
- leaf veiner
- small straight leaf veiner (for sunflower petals)
- small paintbrush
- 6 gum-paste sunflowers (page 164)
- #20 heavy-gauge wires, 6 inches long
- green florist's tape

- block of Styrofoam for drying flowers
- 20 royal-icing petunias (page 152)
- fan cutter
- 22-inch round base, $\frac{1}{2}$ inch thick
- $\frac{1}{2}$-inch-wide blue ribbon to cover the edge of the base
- white glue
- 18-inch Styrofoam disk, 3 inches high
- rolled fondant (page 142)
- small rose-petal cutter
- small rolling pin
- 6- and 14-inch round and 9-inch hexagonal foamcore boards
- $\frac{1}{4}$-inch-thick wooden dowels
- basic buttercream icing (page 139)
- veining tool
- cocoa powder
- pastry bags and couplers
- tips #2, #3, #8, #10, #18, #65, #68, and #352

In advance:

Make the molded-sugar cup and bell. Hollow out the cup, but leave the bell solid. Let dry completely. Flatten the top of the bell slightly by cutting with a sharp knife, then attach the cup to the top with white royal icing. Let dry completely. Use royal icing to glue the Styrofoam ball inside the cup.

To decorate the vase, which should resemble cauliflower, cut out large and small green gum-paste leaves and vein them. Cover the base with small leaves and the lower part of the vase with larger ones. Leave the top third of the vase uncovered. Brush the backs with

Figure 1

a little water to attach them. Pipe small dots of white royal icing above the leaves (figure I). Make a few extra leaves to cover the base of the flowers. Make 25 more large and small leaves to be placed on the 14-inch tier later.

Make 6 sunflowers for the vase. Make 12 large dark-green gum-paste leaves on heavy-gauge wires and let them dry. Tape them to the stems of the sunflowers with florist's tape and insert into the Styrofoam ball in the vase. Pipe green royal icing around the base of the flowers, using the #352 tip, and attach some leaves.

Make the royal-icing petunias.

Use the fan cutter to cut out 6 gum-paste fans, 2 in sky blue, 2 in pink, and 2 in beige. The fans should be about $\frac{1}{8}$ inch thick. Place them on a flat paper-towel-covered surface to dry. Decorate with royal icing, using patterns 1–6.

Cover the base with thinned dark-blue royal icing. Let dry.

To make the beveled layer, outline the bottom of the 14-inch pan on the center of the 18-inch Styrofoam disk. Cut away the excess and sand the disk smooth (see the section on Styrofoam, page 174). Cover it with sky-blue rolled fondant. Attach the bevel to the center of the base with royal icing. Mark 6 equally spaced divisions on the top edge.

Pipe small dots of pale-blue royal icing on the base, using the #2 tip. Glue blue ribbon around the edge of the base.

Using the #10 tip, pipe a bamboo border of brown royal icing around the base of the bevel. Hold the tip at a 45-degree angle and apply steady pressure as you move the bag horizontally. Stop moving the bag at $1\frac{1}{2}$-inch intervals with a push-pull-push motion, then continue moving the bag horizontally (figure 2).

Cut out 215 yellow-orange petals with the small rose-petal cutter. Emboss veins on each petal with the straight leaf veiner and let them dry, vein side up, on a curved surface (figure 3).

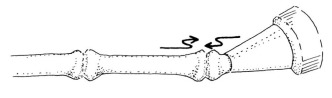

Figure 2

Figure 3

To decorate the cake:

Bake the cakes and let them cool completely. Assemble the tiers on their corresponding foamcore boards. Cover the 14-inch tier with white fondant, the hexa-

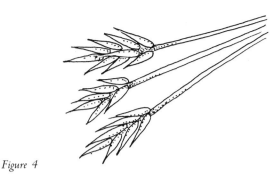

Figure 4

gon with beige fondant, and the 6-inch tier with rose-petal fondant. Insert dowels and stack the tiers on the bevel.

At the top edge of the bevel, pipe a green buttercream bamboo border with the #8 tip.

Tint some royal icing a wheat color by mixing together yellow and brown. Starting at the bevel and with the #2 tip, pipe stems for the wheat stalks at the 6 marks, with 3 or 4 stalks on either side slanting down. Finish the ends by pulling out dots and ending them with points (figure 4). Tint some gum paste

lavender, roll it out, and cut $\frac{3}{8}$-inch-wide strips to fit between the marks. Twist the strips, dampen the ends, and attach them to the points from which the wheat stalks radiate. Make 2 trailing ribbons $4\frac{1}{2}$ inches long in lavender gum paste for each of the 6 sections. Attach them to the ends of the twisted ribbons.

To make the 6 bows, cut $10\frac{1}{2}$-inch strips of gum paste. Twist them into a figure 8, dampen the backs, and attach them above the trailing ribbons (figure 5). Using the #68 tip, pipe green royal-icing leaves in the center of each bow and place a petunia in the icing. Pipe red and white berries with green stems, using the #2 tip and royal icing. Pipe yellow-green royal-icing leaves along the bottom edge above the brown bamboo, using the #352 tip.

To decorate the next tier, cut out 9 2-inch circles of gum paste. Space them evenly around the side of the cake, alternately near the top and bottom, attaching them with a little water. Roll out green gum-paste

Figure 5

stems and attach them to curve between the flowers. Use the #352 tip to pipe green royal icing around the perimeter of the circles and place the rounded end of the curved petals in the icing. Pipe more icing and add another row of petals. Use the #3 tip to pipe brown royal-icing dots in the center of the circles. Use the #2 tip to pipe blue-green dots all over the surface of the tier. Attach the 25 gum-paste leaves to the stems of the flowers with a little royal icing.

To decorate the hexagonal tier, use royal icing to attach a fan to each side, alternately facing up and down. Using the #65 tip, pipe green buttercream leaves around the base and extending up the sides slightly. Use the #18 tip to add elongated stars of wheat-colored buttercream.

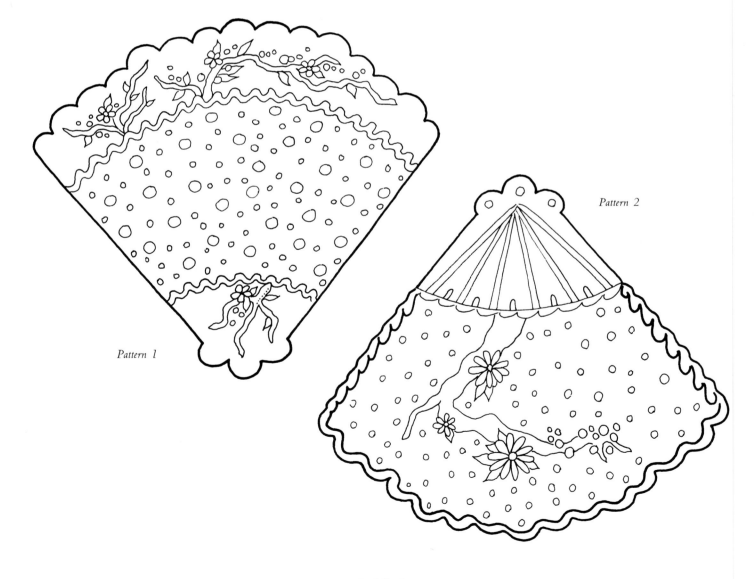

Pattern 1

Pattern 2

To decorate the next tier with cattails, roll out 6 green gum-paste stems 1 inch shorter than the height of the tier. Attach them, slightly curving, to the side of the cake with a little water. Cut out 3 or 4 green gum-paste leaves for each stem, using patterns 7–9. Emboss vertical ridges on the leaves with the veining tool. Dampen the back of the leaves and attach them near the stems, curving them as shown in the photograph to make them look more natural. Roll out 6 pieces of brown gum paste about 1 by $\frac{3}{8}$ inch. Round the ends, then roll them in cocoa to give them a fuzzy appearance. Dampen the backs and attach to the end of each stem.

Finally, secure the base of sunflowers on top with a little royal icing.

Pattern 3

Pattern 4

Pattern 5

Pattern 7

Pattern 8

Pattern 9

Pattern 6

Autumn

Cloisonné Bell

When Christine Provenzano and Terence Mack got married in the country house of a friend in Garrison, New York, they gave out cloisonné bells as favors for the guests. I designed this cake for the couple because of their love of beautiful Asian objects. The unusual shape is ideal for a small wedding.

Serves 60

Cakes:
- 6-inch metal bowl
- 2 8-inch rounds, each 2 inches high
- 9-inch round, 2 inches high
- 11-inch round, 2 inches high

gum paste (page 155)

$\frac{1}{2}$-inch-thick wooden dowel, 18 inches long

cornstarch

cookie sheet

16-inch round base, $\frac{1}{2}$ inch thick

royal icing (page 144)

$\frac{1}{2}$-inch-wide white ribbon to cover the edge of the base

white glue

6-, 8-, and 11-inch round foamcore boards

$\frac{1}{4}$-inch-thick wooden dowels

small serrated knife, such as a steak knife

basic buttercream icing (page 139) or ganache (page 140)

rolled fondant (page 142)

cutters (pages 167–169): $1\frac{3}{4}$-inch circle, petunia, bellflower, and medium and large leaf

2 or 3 small round paintbrushes

brown, red, royal- and sky-blue, moss- and leaf-green, and purple paste food coloring

lemon extract

toothpicks

block of Styrofoam, about 6 inches square

clear piping gel

nontoxic gold powder

pastry bag and coupler

tip #1

Two to three days in advance:

To make the handle of the bell, roll out a thick piece of gum paste about 6 inches long and 3 inches wide. Keep rolling while applying more pressure to one end until it tapers to about $1\frac{1}{2}$ inches thick and resembles a small baseball bat. It should still be 6 inches long; cut off excess if necessary. Sharpen both ends of a $\frac{1}{2}$-inch-thick dowel and brush water along a 6-inch length at one end. Carefully insert the damp end of the dowel into the narrow end of the gum paste, stopping just before the dowel comes through the top (figure 1). Place about 2 cups of cornstarch on a cookie sheet and form it into the same shape as the handle. Make an elongated indentation in the center and place the handle in this well to dry; this will keep the paste from flattening on one side as it dries. Let dry for 2 to 3 days, depending on the dampness in the air, turning the handle occasionally.

Cover the base with thinned white royal icing and glue the ribbon around the edge. Let dry for 24 hours.

To decorate the cake:

Bake the cakes and let them cool completely. Attach the layers to their corresponding foamcore boards with a dab of icing. Spread filling on top of one of the 8-inch layers and top with the second 8-inch layer. Spread filling on the 11-inch layer and top with the 9-inch layer. Insert $\frac{1}{4}$-inch dowels into both tiers except in the center, where the handle will be. Stack the layers.

Using a serrated knife, carve the cake into a bell shape (figure 2). Be careful to shave off only small bits

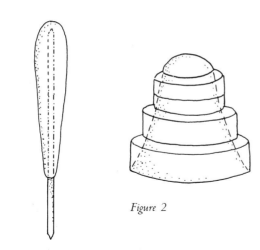

Figure 2

Figure 1

at a time — if you cut away too much, it can't be replaced. It's a good idea to use a turntable to make sure that all sides of the cake are symmetrical.

Cover the cake with a thin coat of buttercream icing or ganache, then with rolled fondant. Place the cake on the icing-covered base.

Cut out circles of fondant, using the round cutter, and cut them in half. Brush the backs with a little water and press them gently onto the cake, cut side down, around the base of the bell. Place some royal-blue coloring in a cup and add a little lemon extract to thin it a bit. Paint the half-circles blue. Reserve the remaining coloring for the top of the bell.

Emboss the entire bell with designs. Using the photograph as a guide, press the petunia cutter into the fondant to make a light impression. Emboss the half-flowers around the top of the bell with the bellflower cutter, as shown in the photograph. Using a toothpick, draw the stems and leaves connecting the flowers. You can also use various gum-paste leaf cutters to emboss the leaf designs.

The handle of the bell is not meant to be eaten, so you can draw the designs lightly on the gum paste with a pencil or a light-colored marking pen. Draw smaller versions of the flowers and leaves that you embossed on the bell.

Use the reserved blue coloring to paint the half-flowers on top of the bell.

In a small bowl, mix brown and red coloring until you get a rust color. Add a little lemon extract to thin

it. Test the consistency and color of this mixture on an extra piece of fondant. Paint the background of the bell and handle around the flowers, leaves, and stems. Don't worry if the brushstrokes show; when the cake is finished, they won't be noticeable. Stick the wooden end of the handle in the Styrofoam to dry while you are painting.

Mix some moss-green coloring with lemon extract, making the color a little lighter than the background. Paint the stems and leaves. Add some leaf green to the moss green and paint the ends of the leaves and stems, as shown in the photograph.

Mix some sky-blue coloring with lemon extract and paint the centers of the flowers pale blue.

Mix a few tablespoons of clear piping gel with about $\frac{1}{8}$ teaspoon of gold powder. Spoon the mixture into a pastry bag fitted with the #1 tip. Using the photograph as a guide, outline all the designs on the bell and handle. Pipe the cloud design (figure 3) all around the background of the bell, handle, and base.

Figure 3

Push a sharpened dowel down into the center of the cake, through the foamcore and into the bottom board. Use a twisting motion to work it through the boards. Mark the point on the dowel where it meets the top of the cake. Remove the dowel. The wooden part of the handle should be $\frac{1}{4}$ inch longer than the mark on the dowel that was inserted in the cake. If the dowel is longer, cut and sharpen it accordingly. Then carefully insert it into the hole made by the dowel. Roll out a small sausage of gum paste to about $\frac{1}{4}$ inch in diameter and wrap it around the base of the handle, cutting off the excess and joining the ends with a little water. Mix some gold powder with lemon extract and paint the gum paste.

Autumn Bouquet

Fall flowers and leaves adorning the cake at an autumn wedding will mark the occasion as the event of the season. Coordinate with the florist to match the colors and types of flower decorations on the cake to the floral arrangements on the tables.

Serves 90

Cakes:
    6-inch round, 3 inches high
    9-inch round, 3 inches high
    12-inch round, 3 inches high
royal-icing decorations (pages 150–154):
    45 small and medium orange and yellow
        chrysanthemums, 25 of them on stems
    30 red and coral roses, 18 of them on stems
    15 orange lilies on stems
    25 yellow daisies, 15 of them on stems
    35 small pale-purple rosebuds on stems
    80 white baby's breath
    35 fall leaves on stems
16-inch round base, $\frac{1}{2}$ inch thick
royal icing (page 144)

$\frac{1}{2}$-inch-wide white ribbon for the edges of the
    base and tiers
white glue
2 3-inch-wide Styrofoam balls, cut in half
2 each 7- and 10-inch separator plates
4 columns 3 inches high
4 columns 5 inches high
red, yellow, orange, moss-green, and brown
    paste food coloring
12-inch round foamcore board
rolled fondant (page 142)
$\frac{1}{4}$-inch-thick wooden dowels
basic buttercream icing (page 139)
pastry bags and couplers
tips #2, #17, and #352

In advance:

Make all of the royal-icing flowers and leaves and let them dry.

Cover the base with thinned white royal icing. Let dry. Glue ribbon around the edge of the base.

Use royal icing to attach a Styrofoam half-ball to the center of one separator plate of each size. Make sure that the plate pegs are facing up. Insert the columns on the pegs, placing the smaller columns on the smaller plate. Insert the stemmed flowers in the balls so that the flowers do not exceed the height of the columns. Use the #17 tip to pipe green royal icing to hold the flowers in place and to cover the Styrofoam.

For the top bouquet, cover the bottom of a third half-ball with foil. Insert flowers and leaves as on the separator plates.

To decorate the cake:

Bake the cakes and let them cool completely. Assemble the bottom tier on the 12-inch board and the other tiers on their corresponding plates. Cover the cake with rolled fondant. Insert the dowels and place the bottom tier on the prepared base. Attach ribbon around the bottom of each tier with dots of royal icing at each end.

Pipe small dots and leaves on stems on all of the tiers, using white royal icing and the #2 tip.

Stack the cakes and place the bouquet on the top tier. Using the #352 tip, pipe green-and-yellow-striped buttercream icing leaves on each tier, up the sides of the bottom tier, and up the columns, as shown in the photograph. Pipe small leaves of yellow buttercream near the leaves, using the #352 tip. Add flowers around the tiers and pipe green leaves around the flowers.

Blue Delftware

The beautiful blue and white designs of Delft pottery have always been a favorite of mine. When a bride-to-be brought a Delft ginger jar with her when she met with me to discuss her cake, I jumped at the chance to incorporate these lovely designs into an unusual and striking confection. You can use a piece of pottery that matches, or you can cover a small, inexpensive ginger jar with fondant and decorate it in the Delft manner.

Serves 150

Cakes:
   6-inch round, 3 inches high
   11-inch round, 3 inches high
   16-inch round, 4 inches high
20-inch round base, $\frac{1}{2}$ inch thick
royal icing (page 144)
$\frac{1}{2}$-inch-wide blue ribbon to cover the edge of
   the base
white glue
rolled fondant (page 142)
6-inch-high vase or ginger jar

small paintbrush
royal-blue paste food coloring
lemon extract
6-, 11-, and 16-inch round foamcore boards
$\frac{1}{4}$-inch-thick wooden dowels
cardboard
leaf cutter
pure white royal buttercream icing (page 139)
pastry bags and couplers
tips #0, #1, #2, #16, and #66

In advance:

Cover the base with thinned white royal icing. Let dry. Glue the ribbon around the edge of the base.

To cover a jar with rolled fondant, roll out a piece large enough to cover the lid. Brush the back with a little water to make it tacky and lay the fondant on the lid, gently smoothing it in place. Cut off the excess so that the lid still fits on the jar. Set aside. Cover the jar in the same manner, cutting the excess from the bottom and top edges. Let dry overnight.

To decorate the jar, replace the lid and set the jar on a turntable. Using the #1 tip and blue royal icing, pipe outlines on the jar as shown in figure 1. To fill in the patterns, mix a little royal-blue food coloring with lemon extract and paint it on with a small paintbrush. Pipe white fleurs-de-lis inside the decorations, using the #2 tip, and add white shells in the smaller areas. Pipe tiny flowers around the middle of the jar with the #1 tip.

Figure 1

To decorate the cake:

Bake the cakes and let them cool completely. Place each tier on its corresponding foamcore board. Cover the tiers with rolled fondant and insert dowels into each tier, including the top to support the jar. Place the bottom tier on the prepared base, then stack the tiers on top.

Trace patterns 1 and 2 onto cardboard and cut them out. Starting with the bottom tier, use the half-circle pattern (pattern 1) to outline the scalloped border with a toothpick, as shown in the photograph.

Outline the elongated curved pattern (pattern 2) onto the middle tier, leaving about $\frac{1}{4}$ inch between each design.

To emboss designs on the top edge of the smallest tier, place the top of the leaf cutter on the edge of the tier. Roll the cutter over the edge onto the side of the cake. Arrange the designs with the widest parts touching. Use the smaller circle pattern to emboss the scalloped edge at the bottom of the tier.

Use royal-blue coloring mixed with lemon extract to fill in the patterns. Brush a little of the color on a scrap of fondant to test the depth of the color and adjust as needed to match the jar. Using a small paintbrush, carefully paint inside the outlines of the patterns on all of the tiers.

Use the floral patterns (patterns 3–8) to trace the flowers, leaves, and curls on the bottom tier, then pipe the outlines in blue royal icing, using the #1 tip. Pipe the same pattern on the base. Fill in the outlines with blue paint.

Using blue royal icing and the #1 tip, pipe a thin rope border around the scallops on the bottom tier, the curved designs on the middle tier, and the leaves and scallops on the top tier.

Pipe smaller flowers on the sides of the top tier and on top of the middle tier, using blue royal icing and the #0 or #1 tip. Pipe tiny white dots in the centers with the #1 tip.

Use white royal icing and the #1 tip to pipe 7 radiating lines in a ropelike motion in the scallops on the bottom tier.

On the top tier, pipe white #2 dots inside the blue area at the leaf points. Inside the scallops, pipe 5 lines with dots on their ends, like 5-pointed fleurs-de-lis.

On the middle tier, pipe stems inside the curved designs, using the #2 tip. Then pipe leaves and petals with the #66 tip, as shown in the photograph. Over-pipe blue lines on top of the flowers and leaves, using the #1 tip. Pipe white dots in the center of each flower.

Pipe shell borders of blue buttercream icing around the base of each tier, using the #16 tip. Pipe vertical shells of white buttercream at the base of the top tier, as shown.

Place the ginger jar on top with a dab of royal icing to hold it in place.

Pattern 1

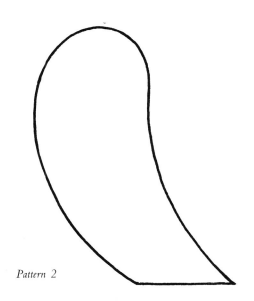

Pattern 2

Patterns 3—8

American Country Quilt

This cake is a tribute to the intricate handwork that I admired on a visit to the People's Place Quilt Museum in Intercourse, Pennsylvania. The tulip bouquet on the top is based on the wonderful, simply designed wooden carvings that are typical of the area. This cake was created for and featured in *Bride's* magazine.

Serves 120

Cakes:
- 7-inch round, $4\frac{1}{2}$ inches high
- 11-inch round, $4\frac{1}{2}$ inches high
- 14-inch round, $4\frac{1}{2}$ inches high
- 25 bamboo skewers, 6 inches long
- green liquid food coloring
- royal icing (page 144)
- cookie sheet
- wax paper
- pink, red, green, and violet paste food coloring
- 16-inch round base, $\frac{1}{2}$ inch thick
- $\frac{1}{2}$-inch-wide white ribbon to cover the edge of the base
- white glue

- 7-, 11-, and 14-inch foamcore octagons
- rolled fondant (page 142)
- 30-60-90-degree triangle and isosceles right triangle
- 18-inch metal ruler
- tracing wheel
- $\frac{1}{4}$-inch-thick wooden dowels
- 3- and $4\frac{1}{2}$-inch wide Styrofoam disks, 1 inch high
- basic buttercream icing (page 139)
- pastry bags and couplers
- tips #1, #2, and #17

In advance:

To make the stems for the top of the cake, tint the bamboo skewers green by placing them flat in a shallow dish, adding a few drops of liquid green food coloring and a little water, and swishing the sticks around until they are tinted. (If you use your hands, your fingers will turn green, too.) Remove the stems and let them dry on a paper towel.

Make the royal-icing appliqués at least 2 days in advance, using the run-in sugar technique (see page 170). Place patterns 1–10 on a cookie sheet and tape a piece of wax paper over them. The flowers, leaves, and hearts for the bouquet on top of the cake are finished on both sides, and some are made directly on the stems. The extra layer of icing strengthens the designs and locks the stems in place.

Using white run-in sugar, make 4 circles $\frac{7}{8}$ inch wide and 4 large and small white stars (pattern 1).

Tint some royal icing green. Outline and fill in 23 2-inch-long leaves, with 8 of them on stems (pattern 2). Make 32 smaller leaves for the top tier and 24 leaves for the bottom tier (patterns 3 and 4).

Tint some royal icing red. Outline 9 tulips on skewers and 18 tulip halves for the bouquet (pattern 5), plus 4 tulips and 4 petals for the top tier (pattern 3). Make 4 large starbursts and 4 stars for the second tier (pattern 1). Make 4 each of the bird wings (pattern 4), and make 64 hearts (patterns 4, 6, 7, 8, 9).

Tint some royal icing pink and make 4 birds facing in each direction (pattern 4). Outline 16 pieces for the circular design on the bottom tier, in pink (pattern 9). Fill in the pink areas and let dry. Finish with red icing, as shown in pattern 9.

Tint some icing violet and make 8 hearts on skewers, 8 hearts without skewers (pattern 10), 4 tulips and 4 tulip petals (pattern 3), 4 circles $\frac{3}{4}$ inch wide, and 64 diamond shapes for the starbursts (pattern 1).

When the appliqués are dry, repeat the run-in process on the other side of the stemmed designs and the tulip halves. Let dry.

To construct the 4-sided tulips, pipe some red icing along the straight edge of a tulip half and attach it to one of the stemmed tulips. Let dry. Turn the tulip over and attach another tulip half. Prop the stem up so the tulip can dry flat. Make a total of 9 tulips.

Cover the 16-inch base with thinned white royal icing. Let dry. Glue ribbon around the edge of the base.

To decorate the cake:

Bake the cakes and let them cool completely. Spread with filling and cut the cakes into octagons (see page 172), using the octagonal boards as templates. Assemble the tiers on their corresponding foamcore octagons.

When quilting rolled fondant, you must cover one tier at a time and quilt it immediately. Otherwise the fondant will crack and the designs will not be clear.

Each tier is quilted in a different manner. The 7-inch tier has 10 equally spaced diagonal lines made with the 30-60-90 triangle, with each side slanting down from right to left (figure 1).

On the 11-inch tier, divide each section into four $4\frac{1}{2}$-inch squares. Using a ruler, lightly mark horizontal and vertical lines in the center with the tracing wheel. Mark the horizontal lines at $\frac{1}{2}$-inch intervals, then mark the top edge, starting at the center line. These marks indicate where to draw the diagonals. The lines go from right to left in the upper-left and lower-right corners and from left to right in the opposite corners. Place the isosceles right triangle flat on the table with the long edge against the cake. Using the marks as a guide, emboss diagonal lines and stop when you reach the center. Emboss all of the lines going in one direction, then turn the triangle and repeat in the other direction. This process creates an embossed diamond shape.

On the 14-inch tier, four of the sections consist of diagonal lines divided down the center, as in a herringbone pattern, and the other four sections have 3-inch circles with diagonal squares inside and four vertical lines on either side. Each section should be $5\frac{5}{8}$ inches wide. Using a ruler, lightly mark the top edge

at 1-inch intervals. Place the right triangle flat on the table. Using the marks as a guide, emboss all of the lines in one direction, then turn the triangle and repeat in the other direction (figures 2 and 3).

When all of the embossing is done, insert dowels in each tier. Place the 14-inch tier on the prepared base. Position the 11-inch tier on the bottom tier so that the corners of the 8 segments line up with the centers of the segments on the tier beneath. The 7-inch tier should line up with the 14-inch tier.

Attach the icing appliqués to the segments on the tiers with a little royal icing, using the photograph as a guide. On the top tier, pipe a snail trail of green royal icing from the tulip stems, using the #2 tip. Place 4 leaves on the tulip stems on each panel.

Attach starbursts of alternating colors on the middle tier. Attach the small violet diamonds to the corners of the stars and add the red star to the center of the white starburst. Attach the circles to the centers. Using the #2 tip, pipe a pink snail trail around the outline of the white starburst.

On alternating sections of the bottom tier, attach the 2 birds facing each other. Attach the wings and the hearts above their heads. Place the 6 leaves as shown in the photograph and pipe a green stem, as on the top tier.

On the other panels, pipe a pink snail-trail circle with the #2 tip. Using the photograph as a guide, place the pink and red designs on 4 sides of the circle, then place the 3 medium hearts in the center and on the top and bottom. Attach the 2 large hearts on the left and right and a small heart in each corner.

Place a small heart in each of the 8 corners of the top tier and the base. Attach a medium heart on each of the 8 corners on top of the middle tier. Place the large hearts on top of the bottom tier.

To make the top ornament, cover the bottom of the $4\frac{1}{2}$-inch Styrofoam disk with a piece of foil, folding the edges tightly up against the Styrofoam. Attach the smaller disk on top and cover them both with green rolled fondant. Insert the stemmed decorations into the disk, starting at the top center with a 6-inch-long tulip. Cut the stems of 4 hearts to measure 4 inches

and insert them around the tulip. Cut the stems of 4 leaves to measure 3 inches and insert them between the hearts.

Slightly farther out and angled, insert 4 more tulips with stems cut to measure $4\frac{1}{2}$ inches, and 4 leaves with stems cut to measure 5 inches, between the tulips.

Insert 4 tulips with 4-inch stems in between the other tulips. Place violet hearts around the top base.

Attach the ornament on top of the cake with a little royal icing. Using the #17 tip, pipe a shell border of green royal icing around the bottom of the disk. Angle 16 leaves around the bottom, attaching them with royal icing.

Finally, use the #17 tip to pipe a shell border of white buttercream icing along all of the edges of the cake, including the divisions between the panels on each tier.

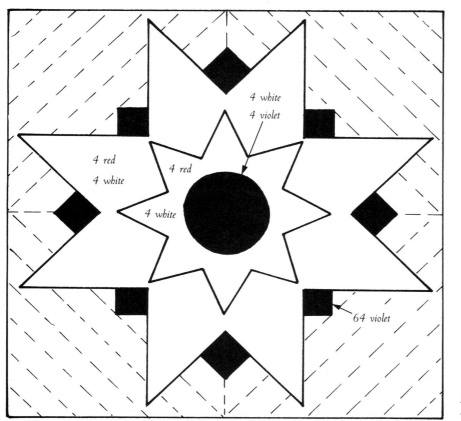

4 white
4 violet

4 red
4 white

4 red

4 white

64 violet

Pattern 1
violet or white, red or white, violet, white or red

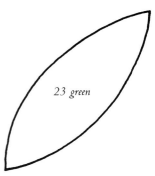

23 green

Pattern 2
Make 15 and 8 on stems

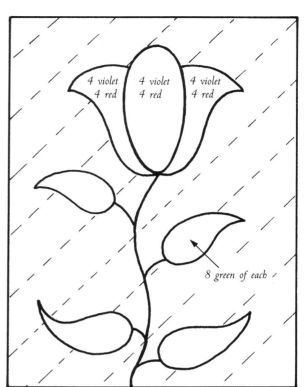

Pattern 3 / Figure 1
violet or red, and green

Within Figure 1: 4 violet / 4 red — 4 violet / 4 red — 4 violet / 4 red

8 green of each

4 red

4 pink of each

4 red

4 green of each

Pattern 4 / Figure 2
pink, red, green

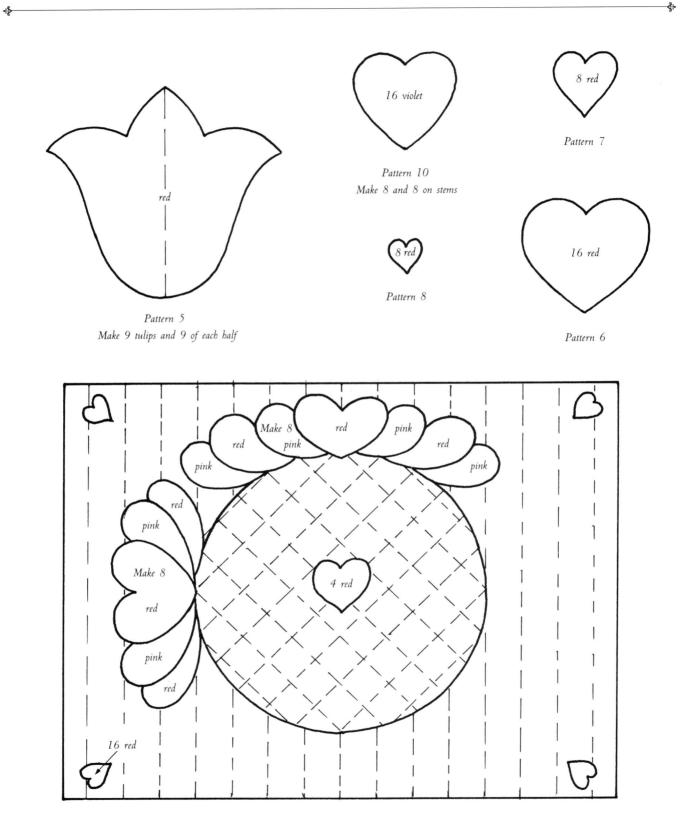

red

16 violet

Pattern 10
Make 8 and 8 on stems

8 red

Pattern 7

8 red

Pattern 8

16 red

Pattern 6

Pattern 5
Make 9 tulips and 9 of each half

Make 8
pink

red

pink

red

pink

red

red

pink

Make 8

red

pink

red

4 red

16 red

Pattern 9 / Figure 3
red, pink

Fan Fare

This cake was inspired by the design on a Japanese kimono. The sponged red coloring gives the cake a rich, crushed-velvet appearance that contrasts with the gold stripes and the delicate flowers.

Serves 130

Cakes:

    6-inch hexagon, 4 inches high

    12-inch hexagon, 4 inches high

    15-inch hexagon, 4 inches high

royal icing (page 144)

black, moss-green, yellow, orange, purple, and
    blue paste food coloring

wax paper

cookie sheet

gum-paste flowers:

    10 Oriental peonies (page 160)

    45 apple blossoms (page 157) and 45 buds
        on wires (page 166)

nontoxic gold, red, and purple powdered
    coloring

small paintbrush

brown florist's tape

6-, 12-, and 15-inch hexagon foamcore boards

rolled fondant (page 142)

18-inch hexagonal base, $\frac{1}{2}$ inch thick

$\frac{1}{2}$-inch-wide red ribbon to cover the edges of
    the base and tiers

white glue

$\frac{1}{4}$-inch-thick wooden dowels

lemon extract

new sponge

clear piping gel

pastry bags and couplers

tips #2 and #3

In advance:

Make 6 run-in sugar fans, using patterns 1–5. The fan on the top of the cake is made of 9 individual pieces attached together in a zigzag formation with royal icing. The other 5 fans (one is not shown in the photograph) are flat and made in one piece. Tint a few cups of royal icing black, pink, and ocher (made from yellow, orange, and a little purple). Tint smaller amounts green and blue, and leave some white. Match the colors to those in the photograph.

    Place the patterns under a piece of wax paper on a cookie sheet. Pipe the outline of each fan with stiff royal icing, using the #2 tip, in the color of the background. Make 2 black, 2 ocher, 1 pink, and one multicolored. Pipe the outline for the design in the fan with the colors needed. Fill in the fan with run-in sugar in the same colors as the outlines. Let dry for at least 24 hours.

    To construct the top fan, place a sheet of wax paper on a cookie sheet. Using the #3 tip, pipe a line

of royal icing along the left edge of a fan piece. Place this edge on the wax paper and stand it up at a slight angle (figure 1). Pipe a line of icing on the left edge of another fan piece and join the second piece to the first piece along the iced edge. Continue adding pieces in this way so that the fan will dry in a zigzag. Reinforce the icing between each piece with another line of icing on top of the first one. Let dry overnight.

    Make the gum-paste peonies, apple blossoms, and apple-blossom buds. When they are dry, dust the edges of the peonies and the insides of the apple blossoms with purple powder. Tape the apple blossoms and buds together into branches, using brown florist's tape.

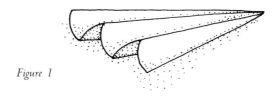

Figure 1

To decorate the cake:

Bake the cakes and let them cool completely. Fill and crumb-coat the cakes (see page 146), and place them on their corresponding foamcore boards. Cover the base and all of the tiers with rolled fondant. Insert dowels in the 2 lower tiers. Glue ribbon around the edge of the base.

To color the tiers and the base, mix red powdered coloring with lemon extract. This mixture should be translucent. Dip a new sponge in the paint and dab it onto the fondant. Cover the cake and base completely. Don't concentrate on one area for too long; the color will start to come off if it's retouched before it dries.

Let dry.

Stack the cakes on the base. Wrap red ribbon around the bottom of each tier and hold it in place with a dab of royal icing. Mix 2 heaping tablespoons of clear piping gel with $\frac{1}{8}$ teaspoon of gold powder. Spoon it into a pastry bag with the #2 tip attached and pipe gold lines on the cake, as shown in the photograph.

Using red royal icing, attach the fans. The fan on top is also supported by peonies in the front and back. Place the peonies on the cake and insert the apple-blossom branches.

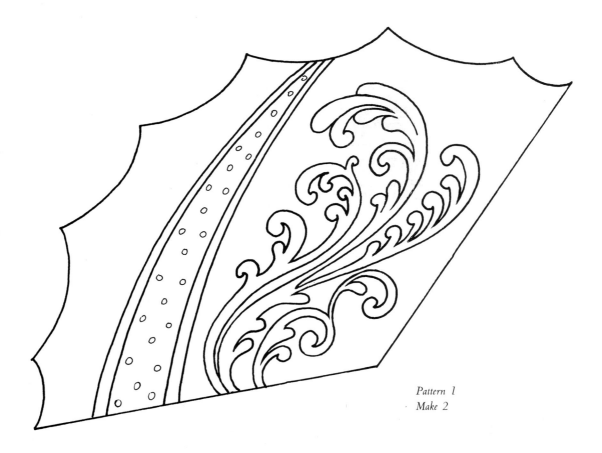

Pattern 1
Make 2

Pattern 2
Make 1

Pattern 3
Make 1

Pattern 4
Make 1

Pattern 5
Make 9

Pas de Deux

Inspiration for wedding cakes can strike at any time. While I was attending a ballet performance, it occurred to me that the pearls and ribbons on the costumes would make a lovely motif for a romantic wedding cake. The pattern is embossed using crimpers and tracing wheels.

Serves 260

Cakes:
- 5-inch square, $2\frac{1}{4}$ inches high
- 7-inch square, $3\frac{1}{4}$ inches high
- 9-inch square, $3\frac{3}{4}$ inches high
- 12-inch square, 4 inches high
- 15-inch square, 5 inches high

gum paste (page 155)
pizza cutter
ridged rolling pin
toothpicks
thin sewing needle
dental floss
nontoxic white, pink, blue, green, yellow, and purple iridescent powdered coloring
lemon extract
small paintbrush

20-inch square base, $\frac{1}{2}$ inch thick
royal icing (page 144)
$\frac{1}{2}$-inch-wide white ribbon for the edges of the base and tiers
white glue
5-, 7-, 9-, 12-, and 15-inch foamcore squares
rolled fondant (page 142)
30-60-90-degree triangle
diamond-shaped crimpers
tracing wheel and zigzag wheel
$\frac{1}{4}$-inch-thick wooden dowels
#26 white cloth-covered wires
pastry bag and coupler
tip #2

In advance:

Make 60 gum-paste loops of various colors and sizes, from $1\frac{1}{2}$ to 3 inches long (see page 155). Make them in different textures, rolling some with the ridged rolling pin.

Use gum paste to make 200 $\frac{1}{2}$-inch-wide pearls and 40 multicolored $\frac{3}{4}$- to 1-inch-wide balls. Let them dry overnight. Insert toothpicks into the balls.

String the pearls, using a needle threaded with dental floss. Double the floss and knot the ends together. Insert the needle through the pearls as you would do with a real string of pearls, leaving a knot at each end of the string. Make 10 strings of different lengths, ranging from 15 to 35 pearls. Carefully paint the pearls with a mixture of white iridescent powder and lemon extract. Let them dry for 24 more hours. Paint the balls various colors in the same manner.

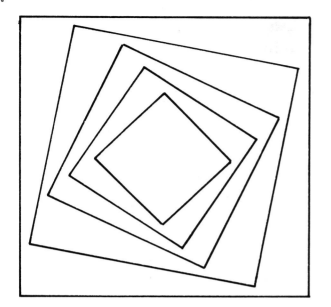

Figure 1
Top View

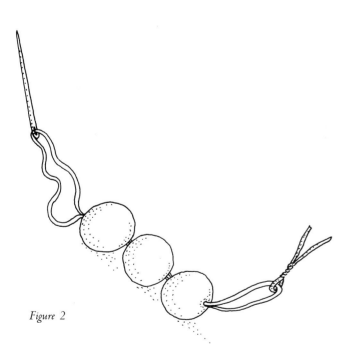

Figure 2

Cover the base with thinned white royal icing. Let dry. Glue ribbon around the edge of the base.

To decorate the cake:

Bake the cakes and let them cool completely. Assemble the tiers on their corresponding foamcore squares. Cover and decorate only one tier at a time, as the fondant needs to be fresh and soft when crimping and embossing. The tiers will be stacked in a spiral, so be sure to outline the top of each tier with the cake pan of the tier above. With the position marked, you will know where to stop decorating.

Cover the bottom tier with fondant and place it on the prepared base. Use the triangle as a guide to emboss diagonal lines in the icing. Using the crimpers, tracing wheel, and zigzag wheel, emboss designs at random angles, as shown in the photograph. Pipe lines of white royal icing, using the #2 tip, to give the design dimension. Pipe similar patterns on the base.

Emboss designs on the other tiers. Paint some of the designs and lines with white iridescent powder mixed with lemon extract.

Insert the dowels and stack the cakes as shown in figure 1. Attach ribbon around the bottom edge of each tier, using dabs of icing. Add the strands of pearls. To hold them in place, bend a medium gauge wire in half and place one end of the string inside. Twist the ends of the wire together into a loop (figure 2). Repeat on the other end of the strand. Insert one end of the strand into the cake and position as shown in the photograph. Pipe a little royal icing on the back of one or two of the pearls to keep them from moving. Be sure to remove the wires before cutting the cake!

After all of the pearls have been applied, attach clusters of ribbon loops around the cake with royal icing. Attach the balls to the cake by inserting the toothpicks.

Golden Wedding Cake

This cake was created for a couple who celebrated their fiftieth anniversary. It would be perfect for a wedding with a white-and-gold color scheme.

Serves 335

Cakes:
- 6-inch petal, 4 inches high
- 8-inch round, 4 inches high
- 12-inch round, 4 inches high
- 16-inch round, 4 inches high
- 20-inch octagon, $4\frac{1}{2}$ inches high

royal-icing decorations (pages 150–154):
- 25 pale-purple hyacinths on stems
- 30 leaves on stems
- 8 grape clusters

gum-paste decorations (pages 155–166):
- 55 roses and buds
- 40 medium and large leaves
- 12 bows, 4 inches long and $1\frac{1}{2}$ inches wide

nontoxic gold and white iridescent powder

lemon extract

medium-sized flat paintbrush

8 columns, 5 inches high

3-inch- and 5-inch-wide Styrofoam balls, cut in half

2 7- and 12-inch separator plates

royal icing (page 144)

gum paste (page 155)

wax paper

22-inch round foamcore board

24-inch round base, $\frac{1}{2}$ inch thick

white glue

$\frac{1}{2}$-inch-wide white ribbon to cover the edges of the base and tiers

8- and 16-inch round foamcore boards

20-inch foamcore octagon

rolled fondant (page 142)

X-acto knife

right triangle

flexible cardboard

tracing wheel

$\frac{1}{4}$-inch-thick wooden dowels

$\frac{3}{16}$-inch gold dragées

gold bride and groom, 3 inches high

pastry bags and couplers

tips #1, #2, #3, #4, #8, #10, #16, and #65

In advance:

Make all of the royal-icing and gum-paste flowers, leaves, and grapes. When they are dry, mix gold iridescent powder with lemon extract and brush the edges gold. Paint the columns gold. Use royal icing to attach a 5-inch Styrofoam half-ball to the center of one of the 12-inch separator plates and a 3-inch half-ball to the center of one of the 7-inch plates. Make sure that the pegs on the plates are facing up. Place the columns on the pegs, then insert the stemmed flowers and leaves into the Styrofoam balls, using royal icing piped from the #16 tip to hold them in place. Be careful not to let the flowers exceed the height of the columns. Place the top separator plates on the columns.

Next, make the 12 gum-paste bows. To make a bow, roll out gum paste to a thickness of about $\frac{1}{16}$ inch. Cut a strip $1\frac{1}{2}$ inches wide and 10 inches long. Brush a little water on each end and fold the ends to meet in the center of the strip. Crumple 2 small pieces of paper toweling and place them in between the loops to keep them from collapsing while they dry. Pinch the center together. Let dry overnight.

To make the center knot, cut a strip of gum paste 1 by 3 inches and $\frac{1}{16}$ inch thick. Brush the back with a

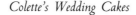

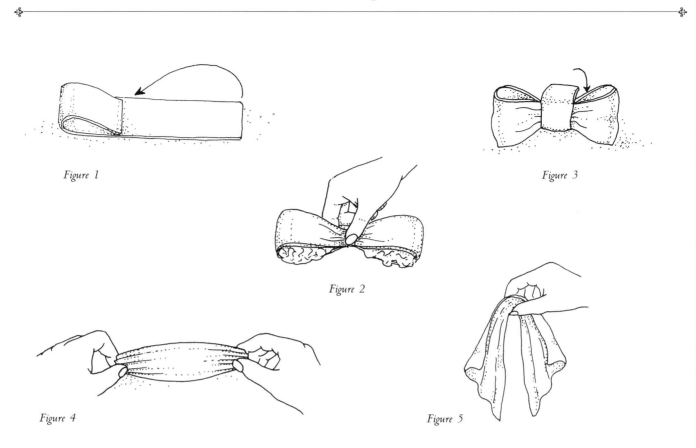

Figure 1

Figure 2

Figure 3

Figure 4

Figure 5

little water and attach it to the center of the bow, with the seam meeting in the back. Let dry 24 more hours.

The top ornament is made of white royal icing on wax paper. Using pattern 1, pipe 3 curved parallel lines, using the #8 tip. Then overpipe zigzag lines with the #4 tip. Pipe a base with the #16 tip. Attach the royal-icing grapes around the surface, then fill in with leaves piped from the #65 tip. Pipe a bow in the center of the top, using the #10 tip. Let dry completely. Carefully turn the design over and repeat on the back to reinforce and strengthen it. Let dry. When the icing is dry, brush it with gold paint.

To make the $\frac{5}{16}$-inch-wide disks, thin a little royal icing slightly until a dot piped from the #2 tip does not come to a point. Pipe 100 dots on wax paper. Let dry. Paint gold.

Glue the 22-inch foamcore board to the bottom of the base and weigh it down with heavy books while the glue dries. This will reinforce the base for this very large cake. Cover the base with thinned white royal icing. Let dry. Glue ribbon around the edge of the base.

To decorate the cake:

Bake the cakes and let them cool completely. Assemble the tiers on their corresponding foamcore boards and on the 2 top separator plates. Cover the 6-, 8-, and 16-inch tiers with rolled fondant. Quilt the other tiers one at a time immediately after covering with fondant (see page 171). Use the X-acto knife to cut a flexible cardboard triangle for quilting. Quilt the sides of the tiers with double lines, $\frac{1}{4}$ inch apart. Place the 20-inch octagon on the prepared 24-inch base. Insert dowels in all the tiers.

Paint the quilted layers with white iridescent powder mixed with lemon extract. Place a gold royal-icing disk at the intersections of the embossed lines, then attach 4 dragées around each disk with dots of royal icing, in a T shape.

Pipe the floral pattern (pattern 2) on the 12- and 20-inch tiers with royal icing and the #2 tip. Let dry. Brush the pattern lightly with the gold paint.

Attach ribbon around the bottom edge of each tier with dots of royal icing.

To make the swags, mark the 12-inch tier with 4 equally spaced divisions and the 20-inch tier with 8 divisions, as described on page 173. Knead an equal amount of gum paste and fondant together. Roll out and cut pieces that are about $\frac{1}{16}$ inch thick, $3\frac{1}{2}$ inches wide, and 2 inches longer than the distance between the marks. Gather and fold the ends accordion-style (figure 4). Brush the backs of the strips at the ends with a little water and attach them to the cake at the marks.

To make the hanging ribbons, cut out pieces of the gum-paste mixture, using pattern 3. With your fingers, gather the center and fold as shown in figure 5 Brush the back with a little water and attach to the cake at the marks.

Secure the bows to the tops of the trailers with a little royal icing. Paint the swags, bows, and trailers with gold paint.

To assemble the cake, stack the tiers, separator plates, and columns. Attach the top ornament with royal icing and surround it with flowers and leaves. Place the bride and groom on top.

Attach the remaining flowers and leaves to the top of the 16-inch tier, as shown in the photograph.

Pattern 1

Pattern 2

Pattern 3
Make 12

Chocolate Fantasia

The layers of this unusual cake are not stacked in the traditional way, but instead are shaped and assembled to create a piece of edible sculpture. I based the chocolate designs on art deco metalwork recently on exhibit at the Metropolitan Museum of Art in New York City, but feel free to dream up creative decorations of your own.

Serves 350

Cakes:
- 5-inch round, 4 inches high
- 6-inch round, 3 inches high, made from the 12-inch layer
- 8-inch round, 3 inches high
- 10-inch round, 3 inches high
- 10-inch round, 4 inches high
- 12-inch round, 3 inches high
- 14-inch round, 4 inches high
- 18-inch round, 4 inches high
- round foamcore boards that correspond to the cake sizes (including 2 10-inch boards)
- 4 foamcore rectangles, 23 by 30 inches
- X-acto knife
- 18-inch ruler

- $1\frac{1}{2}$-inch-thick roll of masking tape
- white glue
- royal icing (page 144)
- eggshell-colored paste food coloring
- $\frac{3}{4}$-inch-wide white ribbon to cover the edge of the base
- white and dark modeling chocolate (page 141)
- variety of flower and leaf cutters (pages 167–169)
- rolled fondant (page 142)
- $\frac{1}{4}$-inch-thick wooden dowels
- small rolling pin
- gum-paste ball tool
- small paintbrush

In advance:

To make the base and the boards for the tiers, arrange one of the 10-inch foamcore boards along with the 12- and 18-inch boards on one of the foamcore rectangles, as shown in figure I. Outline the large shape on the rectangle and the overlapping areas on the round boards, as indicated in the figure. Using an X-acto knife, cut out the large shape and overlapping areas on the round board.

Enlarge the large cutout on another foamcore rectangle (figure I), using the roll of masking tape (see page 173). Cut out this shape, then use it to draw and cut out 2 more from the other rectangles. Glue these 3 shapes together, weighing them down with heavy books as they dry. (This board forms the base for the whole cake; the smaller boards serve as the templates and boards for the individual tiers.) When the glue is dry, add a little eggshell coloring to some thinned

royal icing and cover the top of the base. Let dry. Glue ribbon around the edge.

Cut out the overlapping areas from the remaining round boards, using figure 2 as a guide.

Make the modeling chocolate and let it rest overnight. Roll out the chocolate about $\frac{1}{16}$ inch thick on a surface dusted lightly with confectioners' sugar. Cut out a variety of flowers, layering white and dark cutouts to give the flowers dimension. Use your imagination to create unusual combinations of flowers and leaves. Figure 3 shows a few ideas for flowers.

To decorate the cake:

Bake the cakes and let them cool completely. Fill the tiers and place their corresponding boards on top. Cut the tiers into the shapes of the boards. Cut the 6-inch tier from the remains of the 12-inch tier. Assemble the tiers on the boards and cover with rolled fondant tinted eggshell to match the base. Insert the dowels and stack the tiers on the prepared base.

Roll out long strips of dark-chocolate modeling paste and attach it to the bottom edge of each cake. Brush the back of each strip with a little water if it doesn't stick to the fondant. Press the ball tool into the strips in an even pattern. Roll out long, thin strips of the chocolate and form them into spirals. Attach them to the cake with a little water. Using the photograph as a guide, add curved strips, leaves, flowers, and dots made from small balls of chocolate, brushing them all with water to help them adhere to the cake.

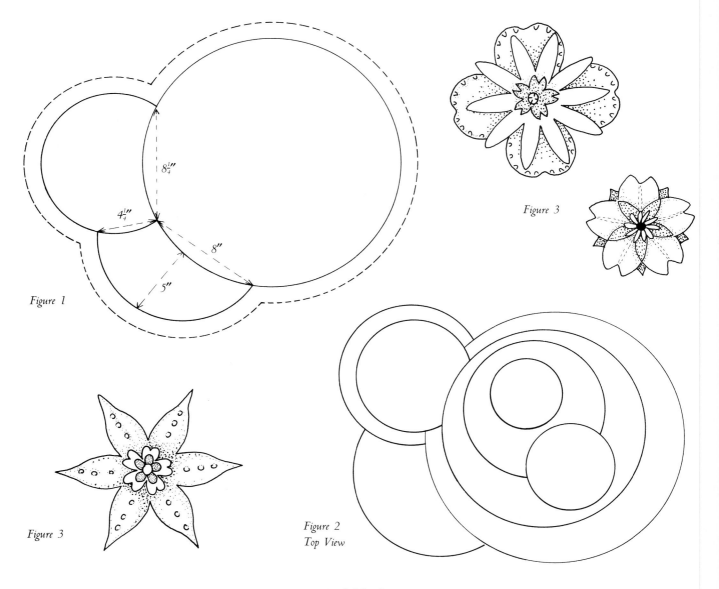

Figure 1

$8\frac{1}{4}''$

$4\frac{1}{4}''$

$8''$

$5''$

Figure 3

Figure 3

Figure 2
Top View

Winter

Valentine Cake

A one-tier, heart-shaped cake is ideal for a smaller wedding. The idea for this design came from layered cut-paper decorations on a beautiful greeting card. The wreath of flowers and birds is made from layered shapes of run-in sugar that add a lush note to the subtle elegance of this simple cake.

Serves 70

15-inch heart-shaped cake, 4 inches high
heart-shaped base, $\frac{1}{2}$ inch thick and $1\frac{1}{2}$ inches
    larger than the cake on all sides (made from
    2 18-inch foamcore squares)
$1\frac{1}{2}$-inch-thick roll of masking tape
X-acto knife
white glue
royal icing (page 144)
$\frac{1}{2}$-inch-wide white ribbon to cover the edge of
    the base

cookie sheet
wax paper
15-inch foamcore heart
small serrated knife
rolled fondant (page 142)
eggshell-colored paste food coloring
pure white royal buttercream icing (page 139)
pastry bags and couplers
tips #1.5, #2, and #14

In advance:

Make a heart-shaped foamcore base, as directed in the section on bases (page 173). Cut out the shape with the X-acto knife and glue the board onto another piece of foamcore. When the glue is dry, cut the second layer around the first. Cover the board with thinned white royal icing. Let dry. Glue ribbon around the edge of the board.

Next, make the run-in sugar decorations. Place the patterns for the birds and flowers (patterns 1–14) on a cookie sheet and cover them with wax paper. Outline the designs for the 2 birds and 45 flowers with royal icing, using the #1.5 tip. Fill in the designs with thinned royal icing from the same tip. Make about 100 partial flowers, such as petals and buds, to add dimension to the whole flowers when placed on top. Let dry completely.

To decorate the cake:

Bake the cake layers and let them cool completely. Add filling, then place the cake on the foamcore heart. Wrap and refrigerate for a few hours. With a serrated knife, carefully shave off the top edge a little at a time to create a curved, pillowlike surface. Crumb-coat the cake (page 146), then cover it with rolled fondant. Place the cake on the prepared base.

Tint some royal icing with eggshell paste coloring. Using the #14 tip, pipe fleurs-de-lis in a grid pattern over the surface of the cake. Pipe small eggshell dots between the fleurs-de-lis, using the #2 tip.

Pipe a generous amount of white royal buttercream on the backs of 13 flowers, using the #14 tip, and arrange the flowers in a heart shape on top of the cake. Add partial flowers, reserving some for the base, and place the birds on top. Attach the remaining flowers around the base with royal buttercream, standing them upright at a slight angle against the cake, as shown in the photograph. Add partial flowers where needed.

Patterns 1–14

Fabergé Topiary

I created this cake for the wedding of Tracy Young and Philippe Content at the Meridien Hotel in Boston. The event was held in a lovely, ornate room decorated with gold accents. Tracy wanted a very unusual and elegant cake, so we decided that a topiary design by Fabergé would make a fitting confection for both the room and the occasion.

Serves 100

2 10-inch square cakes, each 4 inches high
18- and 20-inch foamcore squares, each $\frac{1}{2}$ inch thick
white glue
rolled fondant (page 142)
green and royal-blue paste food coloring
$\frac{1}{2}$-inch-wide white ribbon to cover the edge of the base
pastry brush
gum-paste decorations:
   150 green leaves, 100 large and 50 small (page 166)
   30 small 2-piece roses (page 163)
2 12$\frac{1}{4}$-inch-long hollow plastic tubes, $\frac{3}{4}$ inch wide (found in cake-decorating supply stores)
8-inch-wide Styrofoam egg
hot-glue gun
gum paste (page 155)
veining tool
4 bamboo skewers
block of Styrofoam for drying
royal icing (page 144)
nontoxic gold, white, red, and pink iridescent powdered coloring

small paintbrush
4 3-inch Styrofoam cubes
lemon extract
ragged-edge leaf cutter
long, straight pin
small and medium calyx cutters
trumpet-flower tool
spool of florist's wire
12 sugar molds (page 170):
   8, made in 2-inch-high bell molds
   4, made in 2-inch-wide tart pans
X-acto knife
wax paper
10-inch square of heavy cardboard, $\frac{1}{2}$ inch thick
10-inch foamcore square
$\frac{1}{4}$-inch-thick wooden dowels
cardboard
tracing wheel
$\frac{3}{8}$-inch-wide wooden dowel, 13 inches long, sharpened at one end
pizza cutter
pastry bags and couplers
tips #13, #16, #30, and #352

In advance:

Glue the 18-inch foamcore square, centered, on the 20-inch square to form the base. Tint 1 pound of fondant green and 1 pound light blue, then knead them together until just marbleized. Roll out the fondant until it is about $\frac{1}{8}$ inch thick and large enough to cover the base. Brush the back of the fondant with a little water until sticky. Invert the base on the fondant, little water until sticky. Invert the base on the fondant, then flip both over and smooth the fondant. Cut off the excess around the edge. Glue ribbon around the edge of each board. Brush a little water on the surface with a pastry brush. This will give the fondant a marblelike sheen. Let dry.

   Make the gum-paste leaves and let them dry overnight. Insert one of the plastic tubes about 3 inches into the Styrofoam egg and use the hot-glue gun to glue it in place. Cut a strip of gum paste to fit around the tube and brush it with water to make it sticky. Cover the tube, leaving about $2\frac{1}{2}$ inches exposed at the bottom. Make indentations with the veining tool in the gum paste, as shown in the photograph, to give the impression of bark.

Stick the 4 bamboo skewers into the block of Styrofoam to hold the Styrofoam egg as you decorate. Insert the egg partway onto the skewers, with the tube facing up. Using green royal icing, attach about half of the small gum-paste leaves around the bottom so that they point down and overlap. Then attach the large leaves, overlapping as you work your way to the other end of the egg. When you near the top, let the icing dry for an hour or so, then turn the tree over and insert the trunk into the Styrofoam to keep it upright. Finish the top with small leaves. Let dry.

Make the gum-paste roses and dust them with pink or white iridescent powder. Let dry. Attach them to the leaves on the tree with green royal icing, as shown in the photograph.

Make the legs of the planter from the 3-inch Styrofoam cubes. Cut 12-by-3-inch strips of rolled fondant and brush with water until sticky. Cover the sides of the cubes, leaving the top and bottom uncovered. Then cut 12-by-$\frac{3}{8}$-inch strips of fondant and attach them with water to the bottom edge of each leg. Wrap $1\frac{1}{2}$-inch-wide strips down each corner.

Make 20 gum-paste balls, $\frac{1}{2}$ inch wide, and flatten one side so they resemble gumdrops. Attach the flat side of a ball to the center of the outer 2 sides of each leg. Reserve the rest of the balls for the final decoration. Mix red iridescent powder with a little lemon extract and paint the balls. Let dry.

Cut out 32 white gum-paste leaves, using the ragged-edge leaf cutter. Let dry. Using royal icing and the #2 tip, attach 4 leaves to the legs, pointing diagonally from the red balls to the corners (figure 1). Mix gold powder with lemon extract and paint all of the leaves gold. Paint the strips on the bottom and sides of the legs gold as well.

To make the hanging pearl chains, roll out gum-paste balls ranging in size from $\frac{3}{4}$ inch to $\frac{3}{8}$ inch wide for the small end pearls. You will need 19 pearls for each string. Let them dry for a few hours until firm but

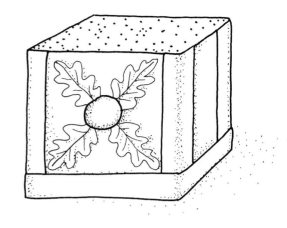

Figure 1

not completely hard. Make a hole in each one with a long, straight pin (such as a hat pin). Make 4 small gum-paste balls about $\frac{1}{2}$ inch wide to top the sugar molds.

Tint some gum paste green to make the calyxes for the pearls. Form the gum paste into a Mexican hat, as described in the section on gum-paste flowers (page 156). Cut out with the medium or small cutter, depending on the size of the pearl. Hollow out the calyx slightly with the trumpet-flower tool, then thin its leaves and attach it to a pearl with a little water. Eleven of the pearls should have one calyx each (5 medium and 6 smaller), and the largest pearl should have 2, one on each side. Insert a pin into the calyx through the hole previously made in the pearl. Let dry completely, then string the pearls on an 18-inch length of florist's wire (figure 2).

Make the sugar molds. Hollow the bell molds until the walls are about $\frac{1}{4}$ inch thick, but leave the tart molds solid. Use the X-acto knife to carve a small hole in the top of 4 of the bells, and flatten the tops slightly by cutting off some of the sugar. Attach 2 of the bells together at their bottoms with royal icing. Let them dry upright. Meanwhile, cover the tart molds, wide side down, with the same marbleized fondant used for the base. When the bells are dry, cover them with the same fondant. Attach the bells to the tops of the tart molds with a little royal icing.

Place the molds on wax paper. Using the #13 tip, pipe a shell border around the base and the center of the molds, as shown in the photograph. Pipe diagonal

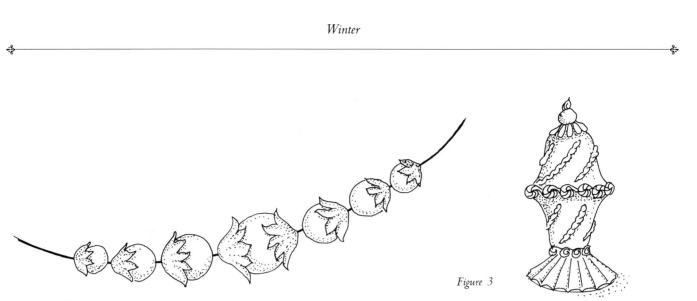

Figure 3

Figure 2

zigzag lines on the bells, using the #2 tip (figure 3). When this icing is dry, paint it gold.

Center one of the 10-inch boards on the base and mark the corners to position the legs. Place the outer corner of a leg at each mark and attach to the board with royal icing.

To decorate the cake:

Bake the cakes and let them cool completely. Because this cake is very tall, it should be constructed in 2 sections, each no higher than 4 inches, with filling in between. Assemble one 4-inch tier on the 10-inch square of heavy cardboard and the other on the 10-inch foamcore square. Crumb-coat each layer (page 146), then roll out a 10-inch square of fondant about $\frac{1}{8}$ inch thick and place it on top of the bottom tier. (That way, when the cake is cut, the bottom tier will also have a layer of fondant on top.) Insert the dowels, except in the center, and add the next tier on its board, making sure that they are perfectly even. Crumb-coat the entire cake.

Covering the cake with fondant will not be as easy as with other, shorter cakes because of its height — the folds in the corners will be very hard to smooth in the conventional way. The best tactic is to smooth the fondant on the top and sides of the cake, then cut the excess off the corners and smooth them. Don't fuss too much, though, because the corners will be covered with fondant strips.

To mark the diagonal lines on the sides of the cake for piping, cut a triangle from a piece of cardboard big enough to reach from the upper-left corner to the lower-right (figure 4). Use the tracing wheel to emboss diagonal lines at 2-inch intervals measured from across the top of the cake.

Insert a $\frac{1}{4}$-inch dowel down through the center of the cake as far as it will go and mark the top of the cake on the dowel with a pencil. Remove the dowel and measure the plastic tube at the end of the tree trunk. Calculate the difference between the tube and the dowel and cut another piece of tube to that length. Insert this tube into the center of the cake as far as it will go. Insert the $\frac{3}{8}$-inch sharpened dowel into the center of the cake, pushing it all the way to the bottom board. Leave it extending up from the cake — it will help keep the tree from tipping over. Place the cake on the legs and secure it with a little royal icing.

Roll fondant about $\frac{1}{8}$ inch thick and cut 10-by-$1\frac{1}{2}$-inch strips with a pizza cutter. Wet the back of one strip and lay it along one of the top edges of the cake, cutting off the excess with a beveled line at the corners.

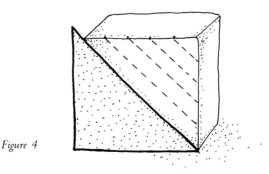

Figure 4

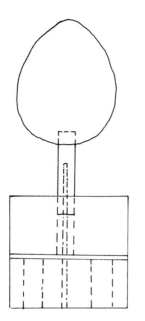

Figure 5

Cover the top and bottom edges. Finally, cut the strips for the corners to fit between the top and bottom edges.

Using the #16 tip, pipe diagonal zigzag lines in royal icing along the embossed lines on each side of the cake. Switch to the #30 tip and pipe large zigzag swags around the cake, as shown in the photograph. Pipe trailers of large shells with the same tip. Let dry, then brush with gold paint.

Tint some royal icing green and pipe leaves on the swags, trailers, and corners, using the #352 tip.

Mark a 6-inch square in the center of the top of the cake. Spread white royal icing in the square, pulling up on the spatula to form peaks. When the icing is dry, paint it gold.

Secure the sugar molds at the corners of the 18-inch base with a little royal icing. Let these dry completely, or they will fall over when you add the pearls.

Insert the ends of the wires with the pearls into the tops of the molds, cutting off excess wire if necessary. Pipe some royal icing on the ends of the wires to hold them in place, and prop up the pearls until the icing dries. Attach the reserved gum-paste balls to the top of each mold. Pipe a little swirl of royal icing on top of each ball. Brush the balls with white iridescent paint and the swirls with gold paint.

Finally, pipe a little icing into the hole in the center of the cake and insert the tree. Spread some royal icing around the bottom of the trunk to hide the separation, and paint the trunk gold.

Art Deco Starburst

This lavender, blue, and white cake was created for a wedding display at Tiffany and Company. The starburst motif echoes the metalwork on the front doors of the famous Fifth Avenue store.

Serves 190

Cakes:
- 5-inch round, $3\frac{1}{2}$ inches high
- 7-inch round, 4 inches high
- 10-inch round, 2 inches high
- 12-inch round, 2 inches high
- 15-inch round, $4\frac{1}{2}$ inches high

18-inch round base, $\frac{1}{2}$ inch thick
large piece of paper, at least 19 inches square
ruler
royal icing (page 144)
purple paste food coloring
$\frac{1}{2}$-inch-wide white ribbon to cover the edge of the base
white glue
wax paper
gum paste (page 155)
gum-paste cutters (pages 167–169): lily petal, Wilton lily, rose-petal, 5-petal flower, Wilton tulip leaf, and one-piece azalea
straight-edged tracing wheel

stiff cardboard
nontoxic white and blue iridescent powdered coloring
lemon extract
small, soft paintbrushes
clear piping gel
silver dragées: tiny seed, $\frac{1}{8}$-, $\frac{3}{16}$-, $\frac{1}{4}$-, and $\frac{3}{8}$-inch wide
3-inch-wide Styrofoam ball, cut in half
aluminum foil
ridged rolling pin
pizza cutter
5-, 7-, 10-, 12-, and 15-inch round foamcore boards
pure white royal buttercream icing (page 139)
$\frac{1}{4}$-inch-thick wooden dowels
pastry bags and couplers
tips #0, #2, and #14

In advance:

To make the pattern for the base, outline the 18-inch round base on the piece of paper and cut out the circle. Fold the circle into sixteenths as neatly and sharply as possible. With a ruler, measure $1\frac{3}{8}$ inches from the curved edge along two of the folded lines on both sides of one section and draw a straight line between the two points (figure 1). Mark the center of the line with a dot. Draw a line to the dot from each corner. Cut out the center wedge through all 16 sections of the circle. Unfold the paper, tape it to the base, and trace the outline on the base. Go over the outline with white royal icing piped from the #2 tip. Fill in the areas outside the outline with thinned white royal

icing. Fill in the rest of the base with thinned lavender royal icing piped from the #2 tip. Let dry. Glue ribbon around the edge of the base.

All of the lavender points on top of the tiers are made of run-in sugar on wax paper, using patterns 1–5. Outline the stars with stiff lavender icing and fill in with thinned icing.

Make the gum-paste cutouts. For the 12 large starbursts, make 12 large shapes with the Wilton lily cutter, 84 large lily petals, and 20 small 3-piece leaves by cutting with the 5-petal flower cutter (figure 2). For the smaller stars, cut 24 one-piece azaleas and 24 leaves with the rose-petal cutter. Score each cutout on

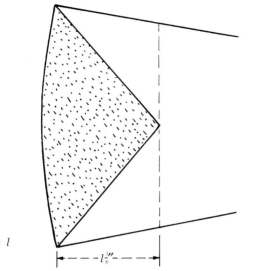

Figure 1

$1\frac{3}{8}''$

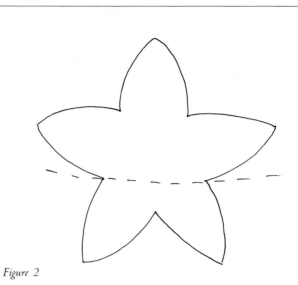

Figure 2

the left side while still soft with a straight-edged tracing wheel to match figure 3. Dry flat on paper towels.

To make the gum-paste cutouts for the top ornament, cut 9 large Wilton tulip leaves and score them
with the tracing wheel. Bend them at a right angle
along the center line, with the scoring on the outside.
To keep the pieces from collapsing as they dry, score
a long piece of cardboard and bend it at a right angle.
Stand it up with the angle facing up and place the
leaves along the edge to dry.

When the gum paste is dry, mix blue and white
iridescent powder with a little lemon extract and paint
the embossed cutout halves light blue.

To construct the large starbursts, place 3 of the
lily-petal cutouts on a sheet of wax paper, all fanning
out from the same point (figure 4). Pipe a little royal

Figure 3

Figure 4

icing on the bottoms of the petals, then attach 4 more petals in between them. Let the icing dry a bit, then add a large lily cutout on top of the 7 petals. Then add a 3-petaled leaf. Let dry.

Using the #0 tip, pipe a line of clear gel along the center line of the petals and leaves and sprinkle with tiny seed dragées. Attach a line of $\frac{1}{8}$-inch dragées along the folds on the folded petals with royal icing. Let dry.

To make the top ornament, cover the bottom of a Styrofoam half-ball with foil. Starting at the top, carefully insert the pointed ends of 4 folded petals into the center of the ball, then add 5 folded petals around them. Pipe royal icing from the #14 tip around the bottoms of the petals and cover the ball with medium and large dragées. Let dry.

To make the stripes for each tier, roll out pieces of gum paste about $\frac{1}{8}$ inch thick, using a ridged rolling pin. With the pizza cutter, cut sixteen $\frac{3}{4}$-inch-wide strips for each tier. Make the strips the height of each tier. Dry flat on paper towels for 24 hours, then place on a flat surface covered with wax paper. Pipe royal icing along one edge of each stripe and attach $\frac{3}{16}$-inch dragées. Let dry overnight.

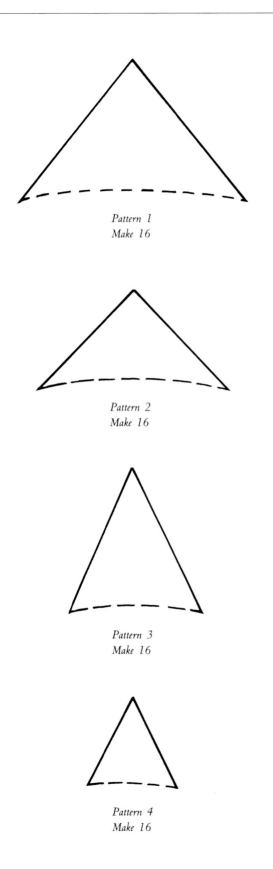

Pattern 1
Make 16

Pattern 2
Make 16

Pattern 3
Make 16

Pattern 4
Make 16

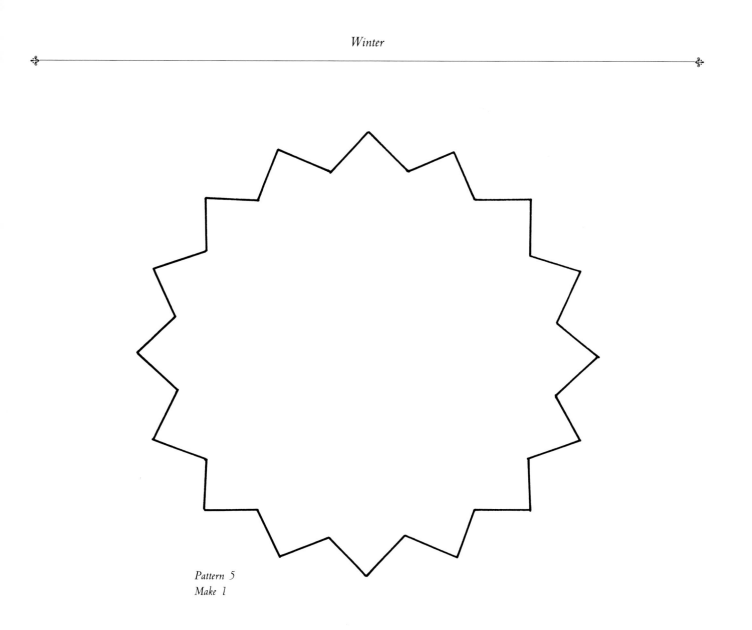

Pattern 5
Make 1

To decorate the cake:

Bake the cakes and let them cool completely. Make sure that the cakes are the correct heights, or the stripes will not fit. Assemble the tiers on their corresponding foamcore boards. Cover them with 2 or 3 layers of pure white royal buttercream icing. Mark 16 divisions on the top 4 tiers, as described on page 173. Insert the dowels and place the bottom tier on the prepared base, using the stars on the base as a guide for the 16 divisions. Stack the remaining tiers, lining up the marks.

Starting with the bottom tier, attach the stripes to the cake with a little royal icing. (The dragées should always be to the right.) Center the stripes above each lavender star on the base.

Attach the lavender stars to the top of the tier, then add stripes to the next tier. Continue until all of the stripes and stars have been added.

Working on a small section at a time, use the #0 tip to pipe a thin line of clear gel around the edge of the lavender stars on the base and all of the tiers. Attach $\frac{3}{16}$-inch dragées in the gel.

Attach the gum-paste cutouts with royal icing, using the photograph as a guide. Secure the top ornament with a little royal icing.

Poinsettia Stained-Glass Cake

A beautiful magnolia lampshade by the master of colored-glass design, Louis Comfort Tiffany, inspired the poinsettia pattern for this winter wedding cake. Piping gel is the perfect medium for creating dramatic decorations that resemble colored glass.

Serves 180

Cakes:
- 9-inch round, 3 inches high
- 12-inch round, 3 inches high
- 16-inch round, 3 inches high

white modeling chocolate (page 141)
red powdered food coloring
pasta machine
pizza cutter
cookie sheet
20-inch round base
royal icing (page 144)
$\frac{1}{2}$-inch-wide red ribbon to cover the edges of the base and tiers

white glue
9-, 12-, and 16-inch round foamcore boards
rolled fondant (page 142)
$\frac{1}{4}$-inch-thick wooden dowels
long, straight pin
brown paste food coloring
red, yellow, green, and blue piping gel *OR* clear piping gel and red, yellow, green, and blue liquid food coloring
small, soft paintbrush
pastry bags and couplers
tip #2

In advance:

Make the white modeling chocolate and tint half of it red with the powdered coloring. Let it set overnight. To make the loops for the bow, run the white chocolate through a pasta machine several times, starting at the widest opening and ending at the #4 setting. Make a few sheets. Repeat with the red chocolate. Place the white chocolate on a cutting board and cut $\frac{3}{16}$-inch-wide strips, as long as possible, with the pizza cutter. Place the white strips on top of the band of red chocolate, lined up straight and evenly spaced (figure 1). Run the striped chocolate through the pasta machine again, on the same setting, to press the white and red stripes together. Using the pizza cutter, cut the chocolate parallel to the stripes, into ribbons 6 to $6\frac{1}{2}$ inches long and $\frac{3}{4}$ inch wide. Form a loop by pressing the ends of each strip together into a point. After making the loops, place them on their sides on a cookie sheet to dry overnight (figure 2).

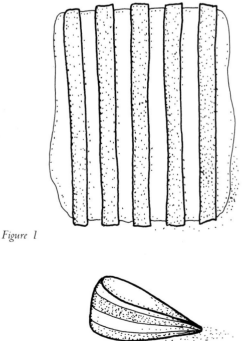

Figure 1

Figure 2

Cover the base with thinned royal icing. Let dry. Glue ribbon around the edge of the base.

To decorate the cake:

Bake the cakes and let them cool completely. Place each tier on its corresponding foamcore board and crumb-coat it (page 146). Cover the tiers with rolled fondant. Insert dowels in the 2 bottom tiers and stack the cakes on the prepared base.

Use pattern 1 to transfer the design onto the cake. Lay the pattern on the cake and outline it with a long pin. This will emboss the pattern in the fondant. Keep in mind that some of the design will go over the edge and onto the top of the cake.

Tint some royal icing dark brown and use the #2 tip to pipe the outline of the designs.

You can use tubes of ready-made piping gel, or you can tint clear gel. If using clear gel, place about 2 heaping tablespoons in each of 4 small containers. Add a few drops of red food coloring to one container; add green, blue, and yellow to the others. The gel will look darker in the container than on the cake, so test the colors by spreading a little of each on a white surface. Add more color a drop at a time, if necessary. Fill 4 pastry bags with the gels.

Using the #2 tip, pipe the red petals of the poinsettia, using the photograph as a guide. Pipe a thick amount of gel at the outer tip of each petal and add some yellow at some points. Using a paintbrush, brush the gel toward the center of the flower, blending the 2 colors slightly.

Pipe all of the green leaves in the same manner as the red petals, adding yellow and blue gel to the green. Pipe yellow dots in the centers of the flowers.

To form the bow on top of the cake, shape soft red chocolate into small balls to attach the ends of the

Figure 3

loops to the cake. Form a ring of loops, then continue to add more loops to fill in the bow (figure 3).

Attach red ribbon around the bottom edge of each tier, holding it in place with dots of royal icing.

Pattern 1

Enlarge 130%

Rainbow Room Cake

I created this cake for a table-setting display at Tiffany and Company in New York City. The display shows a wedding in the Rainbow Room, atop one of the skyscrapers in Rockefeller Center. The cake evokes the art deco style of the room. The stars match those on the tablecloths and, of course, the real ones glistening through the windows.

Serves 350

Cakes:
- 6-inch round, 6 inches high
- 8-inch octagon, 2 inches high
- 9-inch round, 6 inches high
- 12-inch round, 3 inches high
- 15-inch octagon, 3 inches high
- 18-inch round, 4 inches high

royal icing (page 144)
white #20 cloth-covered heavy-gauge wires
wax paper
nontoxic gold powdered coloring
lemon extract
small paintbrush
22-inch round base, $\frac{1}{2}$ inch thick

$\frac{1}{2}$-inch-wide white ribbon to cover the edge of the base and tiers
white glue
round foamcore boards, 1 each 8, 12, 15, and 18 inches, 2 each 6 and 9 inches
$\frac{1}{4}$-inch-thick wooden dowels
rolled fondant (page 142)
trumpet-flower tool
star cutters in various sizes
clear piping gel
medium and large silver dragées
pastry bags and couplers
tip #2

In advance:

Make 40 run-in sugar stars on wires with white royal icing (page 144), using patterns 1–6. Let the stars dry, then repeat on the other side. Paint them with a mixture of gold powder and lemon extract.

Cover the base with thinned white royal icing. Glue ribbon around the edge.

To decorate the cake:

Bake the cakes and let them cool completely. Assemble the tiers on their corresponding boards. Assemble the 6-inch-high tiers as directed on page 146. Cover one tier with rolled fondant and use the trumpet tool to emboss randomly spaced stars around the side of the cake, using the photograph as a guide. Repeat for the other tiers. Insert the dowels and stack the tiers on the prepared base. Wrap ribbon around the bottom of the tiers and glue the ends together with a dab of royal icing or piping gel.

Roll out a small piece of fondant about $\frac{1}{8}$ inch thick. Cut out stars with the star cutters, brush a little water on the backs, and attach them randomly to the cake and the base, as shown in the photograph. (Rolling too much fondant at a time may cause the stars to wrinkle when you put them on the cake. To keep them from drying out, cover the stars with plastic wrap while you are working.)

When all of the stars are attached to the cake, paint them gold. Pipe clear piping gel into the embossed star shapes, using the #2 tip. Attach silver dragées around the cake, using royal icing and the #2 tip. Insert the wired stars in the top and around the cake only after it reaches its destination.

Patterns 1–6

Satin Elegance

The cake that more brides order from me than any other is decorated to resemble a stack of exquisitely wrapped wedding gifts. For this version, the bride-to-be wanted me to reproduce the same bows, pearls, and quilting that she had designed on her gown, and we decided to make the tiers round instead of square.

Serves 175

Cakes:
- 8-inch round, 4 inches high
- 12-inch round, 4 inches high
- 16-inch round, 4 inches high

gum paste (page 155)

nontoxic white iridescent and nontoxic silver powdered coloring

lemon extract

medium-sized flat paintbrushes

royal icing (page 144)

wax paper

$\frac{3}{8}$- and $\frac{1}{4}$-inch silver dragées

18-inch round base, $\frac{1}{2}$ inch thick

$\frac{1}{2}$-inch-wide white ribbon to cover the edges of the base and tiers

white glue

8-, 12-, and 16-inch round foamcore boards

rolled fondant (page 142)

X-acto knife

right triangle

flexible cardboard

tracing wheel

$\frac{1}{4}$-inch-thick wooden dowels

$\frac{3}{16}$-inch gold dragées

pastry bag and coupler

tip #2

In advance:

Make 4 gum-paste bows, 3 small and 1 large. To make a small bow, cut 4 strips of $\frac{1}{16}$-inch-thick gum paste measuring $5\frac{1}{4}$ by $1\frac{3}{8}$ inches each. Make loops from these strips. To make the ribbon ends, cut 4 strips measuring $3\frac{1}{2}$ by $1\frac{3}{8}$ inches each. Cut a notch in one end, then pinch the other end to make a point. To make the larger bows, make strips $5\frac{3}{4}$ by $1\frac{1}{2}$ inches for the loops and $3\frac{3}{4}$ by $1\frac{1}{2}$ inches for the ribbons. Let dry for 48 hours.

Mix silver powder with lemon extract and paint a silver stripe down the center of each loop and ribbon. Pipe a snail-trail line along each edge of the stripes, using royal icing and the #2 tip. On wax paper, assemble the ribbons with royal icing (figure 1). Then attach the 4 loops in between the ribbons. Attach a small gum-paste disk in the center of each bow (figure 2). Add a large silver dragée to each disk.

Cover the base with thinned royal icing. Glue the ribbon around the edge.

Figure 1

Figure 2

To decorate the cake:

Bake the cakes and let them cool completely. Assemble the tiers on their corresponding foamcore boards. Cover one tier with rolled fondant and immediately quilt double lines $\frac{1}{4}$ inch apart, using a flexible cardboard triangle and a tracing wheel (see page 171). Repeat for each tier.

Paint the tiers with white iridescent powder mixed with lemon extract. Insert the dowels and stack the tiers. Attach ribbon around the bottom of each tier with a little royal icing. Attach medium silver dragées at the intersections of the embossed lines with a little royal icing, then place 4 small gold dragées around each silver one, in a T shape.

Attach the bows as shown in the photograph. Prop the bows in place with toothpicks while the icing dries, especially if you must move the cake. Remove the toothpicks at its final destination.

Pineapple Upside-Down Cake

I've always been fascinated by the craftsmanship and varying configurations of chandeliers. When I realized that they look like upside-down wedding cakes, I decided to challenge tradition and make a wedding cake that defies gravity — a cake that's wider on the top than on the bottom. And what better ornament to top an upside-down cake than a pineapple? Actually, this cake is an illusion; only the 2 top tiers are cake. The 3 smaller tiers at the bottom, which are decorated like the rest of the cake, serve as a cake stand.

Serves 125

Cakes:
  12-inch round, $1\frac{3}{4}$ inches high
  16-inch round, 3 inches high
6-inch Styrofoam disk, 2 inches high
8-inch Styrofoam disk, 4 inches high
12-inch Styrofoam disk, 3 inches high
2 16-inch round bases, each $\frac{1}{2}$ inch thick
paper, one piece at least 16 inches square
royal icing (page 144)
hot-glue gun (optional)
$\frac{1}{2}$-inch-wide white ribbon to cover the edge of
  the base
white glue
pink paste food coloring
gum paste (page 155)

tracing wheel
small paintbrush
14 #20 white cloth-covered wires, 7 inches
  long
Styrofoam block for drying
Styrofoam egg, 4 inches high
rolled fondant (page 142)
wax paper
12-inch round foamcore board
pure white royal buttercream icing (page 139)
$\frac{1}{4}$-inch-thick wooden dowels
pastry bags and couplers
tips #1, #1.5, #2, #3, #15, #16, #17, #20,
  and #199

In advance:

The bottom 3 tiers of this cake are 6-, 8-, and 12-inch Styrofoam disks decorated with royal icing. You can decorate them well in advance of the wedding. Although royal icing is very strong when dry, I recommend using hot glue to join the Styrofoam disks.

Use a marking pen to outline each disk centered on each successive disk, plus one of the bases, to help line up the layers when stacking them. Then outline each disk on a piece of paper, including the 16-inch base and the 12-inch cake pan. Cut out each paper circle and fold it into sixteenths. Unfold the circles.

Cover the sides of each disk with 2 layers of slightly thinned white royal icing. Let one layer dry before adding the next. Cover the top of each layer with a thicker layer of icing, but only on the outside of the marked circle. This will actually be the bottom of each tier. Let dry.

Place the paper circles on the corresponding disks and mark each section with a pencil at the top and bottom of the disk.

Glue the 6-inch Styrofoam disk to the center of the base. If the base has foil on it, remove it from inside the marked circle for a better seal. Cover the rest of the base with thinned white royal icing. Glue ribbon around the edge of the base.

All of the decorations are done in white royal icing, except where pink is noted. Tint some icing pink for these.

To decorate the 6-inch tier:

Pipe a white royal-icing shell border around the bottom edge, using the #199 tip. Pipe a rope border above each shell with the #2 tip (figure 1).

Starting at the top of the tier, use the #3 tip and

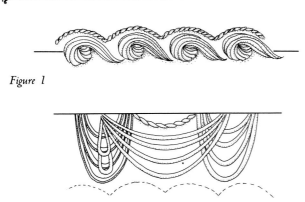

Figure 1

Figure 2

pink royal icing to pipe 4 strings, I inch wide, at every other mark (8 marks in all). The longest string should stop just above the top of the shell border. Using the #2 tip, overpipe the pink strings with white strings.

Pipe 4 longer white strings from the center of one set of strings to the next. Then pipe loops at the end of each long string and add a rope above the strings with the #2 tip (figure 2).

Using the #15 tip, pipe a rosette over each shell on top of the shell border. Pipe a scallop between the rosettes with the same tip. Make cushions between the scallops on the rosettes by piping 5 lines with the #2 tip in one direction, then crisscrossing the lines in the opposite direction. Overpipe the first lines with the #1.5 tip, then with the #1 tip. Each set of lines should be slightly shorter to create a puffy effect (figures 3–6).

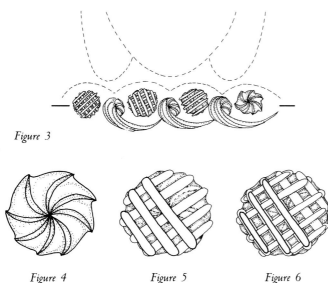

Figure 3

Figure 4   Figure 5   Figure 6

Pipe pairs of opposite-facing scrolls on the base from the tails of the scallops to the edge of the base, using the #17 tip. Pipe a smaller elongated shell between the scrolls. Use the #2 tip to pipe 3 small shells on top of the center shell. Using the #2 tip, pipe pink hearts in between the shells (figure 7). Pipe a shell border with the #17 tip around the edge of the base.

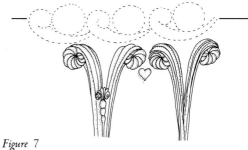

Figure 7

To decorate the 8-inch tier:

Glue on the next tier, lining up the marks with those on the bottom tier.

Using the #17 tip, pipe 8 scrolls at every other mark along the bottom edge. Overpipe a #16 scroll, stopping about $\frac{1}{2}$ inch before the next scroll.

Pipe a #2 rope border above the scrolls, following their contours. Pipe a rope around the bottom of the circular part of each scroll. With the same tip, pipe 4 strings from the bottom of the scrolls and pipe 2 loops in between the strings. Pipe a pink dot in the center of each scroll. End with a #15 rosette over the ends of the string (figure 8).

Figure 8

Pipe 16 arches from the top halfway down the tier, using the #3 tip. Switch to the #2 tip and overpipe ropes on the arches. Pipe dots along the insides of the arches. Pipe alternating bows and 3 dots on the ends of the arches. Overpipe the bows with the #1.5 tip.

Figure 9

Pipe 4 strings inside and outside the arches and small pink hearts between them (figure 9).

To decorate the 12-inch tier:

Glue on the third tier, lining up the marks. Let dry. Turn the entire cake and base upside down (place one hand under the base and the other hand on top of the tier).

First, pipe a rope border along the top edge with the #2 tip. Begin decorating at the marks that line up with the hearts on the 8-inch tier. Use the #2 tip to pipe a row of 3 strings, measuring $2\frac{1}{2}$ inches total. Pipe

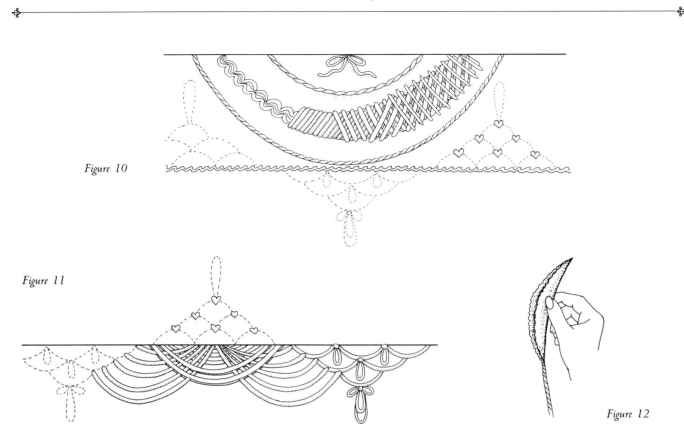

Figure 10

Figure 11

Figure 12

2 strings below and between the strings above, and one in the center below the last 2, ending about halfway down the side. Repeat, piping strings at every other mark. Make loops at the end of the last strings, stopping about $\frac{3}{4}$ inch from the bottom of the tier. Let dry.

Invert the cake again. Starting $\frac{3}{4}$ inch from the mark above one of the string arrangements, use the #15 tip to pipe a zigzag garland to $\frac{3}{4}$ inch from the next mark. The top should also be $\frac{3}{4}$ inch from the bottom edge. Pipe 8 garlands around the tier.

To make the garland cushions, use the #3 tip to pipe diagonal lines next to each other over the garlands. Pipe this layer over all of the garlands. Repeat these lines in the opposite direction on all of the garlands, leaving a #3 space between each line. Overpipe the lines in both directions in the same order on all of the garlands, using the #2 tip.

Pipe a rope border above and below each cushion, using the #2 tip. Pipe bows between the cushions. Pipe 6 strings extending below the edge of the tier below the cushions, as you did when the cake was upside down. Pipe loops between and below the

strings. Pipe pink hearts at the intersections of the upside-down strings, and pink dots on the right-side-up strings (figure 10).

Still using the #2 tip, pipe 5 strings below the string arrangements under the cushions. Then make sets of 5 strings connecting the 2 kinds of string arrangements. Overpipe the 5 strings in the center (figure 11).

To make the pineapple:

Use patterns 1 and 2 to cut gum-paste leaves with the tracing wheel, which will give the leaves a serrated edge. Brush a little water along the center of each leaf and press on a slightly curved white wire (figure 12). Pinch the paste slightly along the wire to give it a fold. Place the wires in Styrofoam to dry overnight.

Cut off 1 inch on the wide end of the Styrofoam egg horizontally. Cover the bottom with foil. Cover the egg with rolled fondant, brushing the Styrofoam first with a little water to help the fondant adhere.

Using off 1 inch on the #2 tip and white royal icing, pipe 8 evenly spaced vertical lines on the egg from the top to the bottom. Pipe 3 even horizontal strings between the lines (figure 13). From the center of the lowest points on the strings, pipe 3 more strings. Then pipe loops between the strings. Pipe pink hearts at the tops of the loops (figure 14). Attach the leaves by inserting the wires into the top of the pineapple.

Make 40 white royal-icing scrolls, using pattern 3 under wax paper, with the #17 tip. Let them dry, then pipe the backs. Let dry.

Figure 13   *Figure 14*

To decorate the cake:

Bake the cakes and let them cool completely. Assemble the 12-inch cake on the 12-inch foamcore board, and the 16-inch cake on the second 16-inch base. Cover with pure white royal buttercream icing. Insert the dowels in the large tier and stack the tiers on the stand formed by the bottom 3 tiers.

To decorate the 16-inch tier:

At the 8 marks between the cushions, attach 5 royal-icing scrolls under the base with royal icing, so that the center one is straight and the other 4 fan out slightly (figure 15).

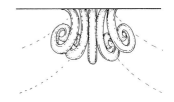

Figure 15

Starting directly above the 5 curls, pipe 19 vertical lines, with the longest line in the center and 9 descending lines on each side. Use the #15 tip and pipe the lines next to each other. The 5 center lines should continue onto the tops of the curls. Make each line $\frac{1}{8}$ inch shorter than the one before it.

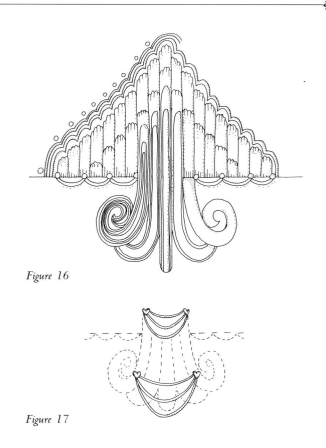

Figure 16

Figure 17

Overpipe the first 13 lines, making each line $\frac{1}{2}$ inch shorter than the one below. With the #6 tip, pipe 5 vertical lines $\frac{1}{2}$ inch below the last #15 line, onto each scroll. Continue adding lines in decreasing sizes on the scrolls, first with the #3 tip, then with the #2 tip.

Pipe a double line with the #2 tip, following the contour of the top edge of the #15 vertical lines, then add dots at each intersection of the scallops. At the bottom of the vertical lines on each side of the scrolls, pipe 3 strings (figure 16). Pipe 2 sets of 3 strings on top of the scrolls. Pipe pink hearts at the ends of each set of strings (figure 17).

Starting at the top edge of the tier, between the vertical lines, use the #3 tip to pipe 7 scalloped strings — 3 down, 1 across, and 3 up again, as shown in the photograph. Pipe 2 strings extending just below the tier. Pipe a rope above the strings, following their contours. Overpipe the strings with the #1.5 tip.

Pipe a small zigzag border around the top edge of the cake, using the #3 tip. On the top edge of the tier, above the scalloped strings, pipe 3-inch-wide buttercream zigzags with the #15 tip, tapering the ends.

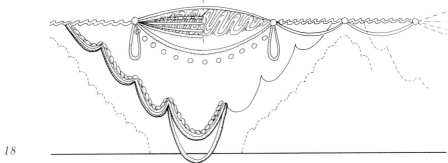

Figure 18

Pipe 6 alternating #2 and #3 strings over the tapered zigzags. Using the #3 tip, pipe a string below each zigzag and add dots along the bottom of the line. Pipe 2 equal-length strings between each zigzag, then pipe loops on both ends of the zigzags with the #2 tip. Add pink dots above the loops and between the strings (figure 18).

To decorate the top (12-inch-cake) tier:

Use the #199 tip to pipe a line of buttercream around the base. Pipe dots above and below the line, using the #3 tip. With the #17 tip, overpipe tapered buttercream zigzags on the line in the spaces between the zigzags on the tier below. Switch to the #3 tip and overpipe 5 royal-icing strings across the zigzags, with the fifth line lying on the top of the tier below. Pipe dots on the second and fifth lines. Pipe a #3 string on the top of the 16-inch tier, connecting the 2 tapered zigzags (figure 19).

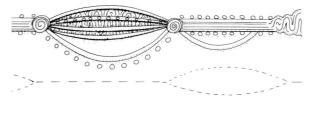

Figure 19

On the top edge, pipe a scroll with the #20 tip, starting at the center of the zigzag below (figure 20). Overpipe it with the #17 tip, then the #15 tip, followed by the #3 and #2 tips (figures 21–23). On top of each scroll, overpipe with the #6, #3, and #2 tips,

Figure 20

Figure 21

Figure 22

Figure 23

letting the icing dry after each tip. Pipe a #2 rope on top (figure 24).

On the second scroll in front, overpipe on top as above, using the #6, #3, and #2 tips (figure 25). Pipe a #2 zigzag under the scrolls, following their contour. Pipe a string over the zigzag and one below it, using the same tip. Pipe a loop under the curves. Add a pink heart at the end of the loop (figure 26).

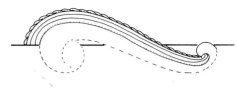

Figure 24

Figure 25

Figure 26

Place the pineapple on top of the cake. Use the #20 tip to pipe scrolls around the base of the pineapple, extending onto the top of the cake. Finish by piping additional scrolls with the #6 and #17 tips (figure 27).

If you are delivering this cake, add the top tiers only after it reaches its destination. Tape the 16-inch tier to a piece of Styrofoam that is higher than the depth of the decorations yet smaller than 16 inches.

Figure 27

Pattern 1
Make 9

Pattern 2
Make 9

Pattern 3
Make 40

Basic Recipes

Colette's Chocolate Cake

This deliciously rich cake is moist and very easy to make. It's my most popular cake.

Yields 6 cups of batter, enough to serve 20

2 cups sugar
$2\frac{1}{2}$ cups all-purpose flour
1 cup unsweetened cocoa
1 cup vegetable shortening
1 teaspoon salt
2 teaspoons baking powder

1 teaspoon baking soda
2 eggs, room temperature
1 cup milk, room temperature
1 teaspoon almond extract
1 teaspoon vanilla extract
1 cup hot, strong coffee

Preheat oven to 325 degrees F. Grease the sides and bottom of two 9-inch pans with shortening, then dust with flour. In a large mixing bowl, combine all ingredients except the coffee. Mix at slow speed until blended, scraping the sides occasionally with a rubber spatula. Slowly add the coffee while mixing on low.

Mix for about 1 minute, or until smooth. Do not overbeat. Place in the prepared pans. Bake for about 45 minutes or until a toothpick inserted in the center comes out clean. Cool in the pans on wire racks for about 20 minutes, then invert onto racks and remove pans. Cool completely.

Snow White Cake

This deliciously light, pure white cake, which is not too sweet, is perfect for any wedding. To make a lemon cake, add lemon extract instead of vanilla and 2 teaspoons of lemon zest.

Yields 6 cups of batter, enough to serve 20

$\frac{3}{4}$ cup vegetable shortening
$1\frac{1}{2}$ cups sugar
2 teaspoons vanilla extract
$2\frac{3}{4}$ cups sifted cake flour

$\frac{1}{2}$ teaspoon salt
4 teaspoons baking powder
1 cup milk, room temperature
4 egg whites, room temperature

Preheat oven to 350 degrees F. Grease and flour the sides and bottom of two 9-inch cake pans. In the large bowl of an electric mixer, cream shortening until light and airy. Slowly add 1 cup of sugar, continuously beating until fluffy. Add vanilla.

In a small bowl, sift the dry ingredients together. Add 1 tablespoon of the dry ingredients to the shortening mixture and mix well. Then add 1 tablespoon of milk to the shortening mixture and mix well. Continue adding the dry ingredients alternately with the mix, blending well after each addition, until thoroughly combined. Do not overmix.

In another bowl, beat egg whites until fluffy. Slowly add $\frac{1}{2}$ cup of the sugar and beat until stiff, shiny peaks form. Gently fold the egg whites into the batter until blended, being careful not to overmix. Place in the prepared pans and bake about 20 minutes or until a toothpick inserted in the center comes out clean. Let the cakes cool in the pans for about 20 minutes, then invert onto wire racks and remove pans. Cool completely.

Basic Buttercream

Very easy to make, basic buttercream is good for icing a cake and for piping decorations and borders. It will stay fresh for 2 days without refrigeration and can be stored in the refrigerator for up to 2 weeks.

Yields 5 cups

I cup butter or margarine, room temperature
$\frac{1}{2}$ cup milk, room temperature

2 teaspoons vanilla extract or other desired
    flavoring
2 pounds confectioners' sugar

Combine all ingredients in large mixing bowl and mix at slow speed until smooth. If stiffer icing is needed or the weather is very warm, add a little extra sugar. This recipe makes enough to fill and cover a 2-layer 9-inch cake.

Chocolate Buttercream

For a simple chocolate buttercream that's good for piping, add $\frac{1}{2}$ cup of unsweetened cocoa and 2 tablespoons of cold, strong coffee to the basic buttercream recipe.

Pure White Royal Buttercream

When you need a pure white icing, this buttercream is perfect for making piped flowers and other decorations. It is similar to basic buttercream, but the meringue powder makes it sturdier and slightly stiffer. This icing will stay fresh in the refrigerator for about a month.

Yields 5 cups

$\frac{1}{4}$ cup meringue powder
2 pounds confectioners' sugar
$1\frac{1}{2}$ cups vegetable shortening

6 tablespoons water
I tablespoon clear flavoring (a tinted flavoring
    will change the color of the icing)

Combine all ingredients in a bowl and mix at slow speed until smooth. Add a few drops of water, if needed. This recipe makes enough to fill and cover a 2-layer 9-inch cake.

Meringue Buttercream

This delicious, fluffy icing has a lighter taste than basic buttercream but is somewhat more complicated to make. I don't recommend making this icing in very hot and humid weather. It can be stored at room temperature for 2 days or refrigerated for 10 days.

Yields 4½ cups

I pound (4 sticks) unsalted butter, softened but cool
I cup granulated sugar
¼ cup water

candy thermometer
5 large egg whites, room temperature
½ teaspoon cream of tartar
2 teaspoons flavoring or liqueur

Beat the butter until smooth and set aside. In a small saucepan, combine ¾ cup of sugar and the water. Stir until the sugar is dissolved. Slowly heat the mixture, stirring constantly, until it starts to bubble. Reduce heat to low and insert a candy thermometer. Do not continue to stir.

In the large bowl of an electric mixer, beat the egg whites at medium speed until foamy. Add cream of tartar and beat at high speed until soft peaks form. Gradually add the ¼ cup of sugar and beat until stiff peaks form.

Meanwhile, boil the sugar mixture until it reaches 248–250 degrees F on the candy thermometer. *Do not*

let the temperature go above 250 degrees F. Turn off the heat and immediately pour the contents into a glass measuring cup to stop the sugar from cooking. Pour a little of the sugar mixture onto the egg whites and beat at slow speed. Slowly add the rest of the sugar. Beat at high speed for 2 minutes, then reduce the speed to low until the mixture is cool.

Add the butter, I tablespoon at a time, to the egg-white mixture, beating continuously on low until all of the butter is incorporated and the mixture is smooth. Add the flavoring. This recipe will fill and cover a 2-layer 9-inch cake.

Chocolate Ganache

For chocolate lovers, this is the most delicious icing for filling and covering a cake. You can use it as a glaze when freshly made or beat it to thicken it for spreading. It is very stable and perfect for crumb-coating a cake to be covered with rolled fondant, although it will soften in very hot weather. You can store it safely at room temperature for 2 days and refrigerate it for up to a week.

Yields 2 cups

12 ounces semisweet chocolate (use chips or cut blocks into small pieces)

8 ounces heavy cream
2 teaspoons flavoring or liqueur (optional)

Place the chocolate in a large metal or glass bowl. Heat the cream in a saucepan just to the boiling point. Pour the cream over the chocolate, making sure that all of the chocolate is covered. Cover the bowl and let stand for 5 to 10 minutes.

Whisk the chocolate until dark and shiny, then cool to room temperature. To thicken, beat cooled icing with a hand mixer for a few minutes. It's best if used after 12 hours.

This recipe yields enough to fill and cover an 8-inch cake, 3 inches high.

Modeling Chocolate

Modeling chocolate has a consistency similar to that of Tootsie Rolls or soft gum paste, although it doesn't dry as hard as the latter and is tastier on a cake. You can use it to make bows, flowers, and leaves or to cover a cake. Running it through a pasta machine is easier than rolling it out with a rolling pin.

The following recipes each yield about 1 cup.

Dark Modeling Chocolate

10 ounces semisweet chocolate (use chips or
    break blocks into small pieces)
4 ounces light corn syrup

Melt the chocolate in a bowl over a saucepan of hot but not boiling water. Stir in the corn syrup; the chocolate will start to stiffen almost immediately. Stir until the ingredients are completely combined. Wrap in plastic until cool.

The paste will seem hard, but it will soften from the warmth of your hands when you start to work with it. Roll it out with a rolling pin, or run it through a pasta machine starting at the widest opening, then through smaller openings until it reaches the thickness you want.

White or Colored Modeling Paste

10 ounces white or colored chocolate-coating
    disks
4 ounces corn syrup

Follow the same directions as above.

Rolled Fondant

Rolled fondant is a sweet, elastic icing that is easy and versatile. It's rolled out with a rolling pin, draped over the cake, and smoothed with the hands. It has become very popular in the United States since its recent introduction from England. Fondant gives a cake a beautiful porcelainlike surface on which to decorate. It's perfect for hot, humid weather because it won't melt and keeps a cake fresh for 2 days at room temperature. You can buy premade fondant at cake-decorating supply stores; it works very well.

Yields 2 pounds, enough to cover a 9-inch cake, 4 inches high

2 pounds confectioners' sugar
$\frac{1}{4}$ cup cold water
1 tablespoon unflavored gelatin
$\frac{1}{2}$ cup glucose (found in cake-decorating stores)

OR white corn syrup
$1\frac{1}{2}$ tablespoons glycerine (found in cake-decorating stores)
1 teaspoon flavoring (vanilla will give the fondant an off-white color)

In a large bowl, sift the sugar and make a well in the center. Pour the water into a small saucepan and sprinkle the gelatin on top to soften for about 5 minutes. Heat the gelatin and stir until dissolved and clear. *Do not boil.* Turn off the heat and add the glucose or syrup and glycerine, stirring until well blended. Add flavoring. Pour into the well of sugar and mix until all of the sugar is blended. Knead the icing with your hands until it becomes stiff. If the mixture is sticky, add small amounts of confectioners' sugar.

Shape the mixture into a ball, wrap it tightly in plastic wrap, and place it in an airtight container. This icing works best if allowed to rest at room temperature for about 8 hours, particularly if the weather is humid. Fondant may be refrigerated or frozen for longer storage, but you must bring it to room temperature to soften before rolling. Do not refrigerate a cake covered with fondant, however, because the fondant will become gummy when brought back to room temperature.

To color fondant, add small amounts of paste food coloring and knead it until the color is even. Add just a little coloring at a time so the color isn't too dark. You can always make it darker, but you can't make it lighter.

To paint fondant with a liquid coloring once it's on a cake, first roll out a small piece of extra fondant and brush or sponge on the color to make sure it has the correct consistency and tint. Adding lemon extract to liquid or paste colors helps them evaporate quickly. The paint should be translucent, but not too thick. Then brush or sponge the coloring on the cake. Cover the surface as thoroughly as possible, but do not paint over wet areas or the fondant will become gummy and the color will lift off. Let the color dry, then retouch if necessary.

To cover a cake with fondant:

Dust a clean, smooth surface with cornstarch or confectioners' sugar to prevent sticking and roll the fondant with a rolling pin until it is about $\frac{1}{4}$ inch thick. Make sure that the fondant is large enough to fit over the top and sides of the cake. Slide both hands under the fondant and carefully center it on top of a cake that has been freshly iced with buttercream. The icing will make the fondant adhere to the cake.

To cover other edible surfaces, such as sugar molds, brush the back of the rolled fondant with a little water to make it sticky. When covering Styrofoam, dampen the Styrofoam with water before covering it with fondant.

Dust your hands with cornstarch and smooth the fondant, starting at the top and working down the

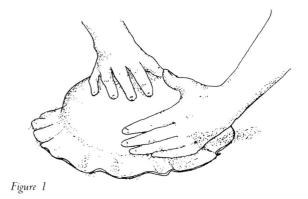

Figure 1

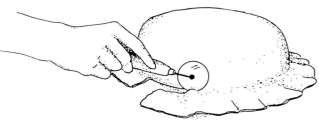

Figure 2

sides until the entire surface is even and flat (see figure I). Cut off the excess fondant around the bottom of the cake, using a pizza cutter or a sharp knife (see figure 2). You can reuse the extra fondant.

If you plan to emboss a design in the fondant with crimpers or a tracing wheel, you must do it immediately. The surface of the fondant dries quickly and may cause the embossing to wrinkle if you wait too long.

You can then decorate the cake with buttercream or royal icing.

Chart for Rolled Fondant

The following table will help you determine how much fondant you need to cover various sizes of cakes, all about $3\frac{1}{2}$ inches high. At least $\frac{1}{2}$ pound will be trimmed away and may be reused.

cake	pounds of fondant
round, octagon, or hexagon	
6-inch	$1\frac{1}{2}$
8-inch	2
10-inch	$2\frac{1}{2}$
12-inch	3
14-inch	4
16-inch	5
square	
6-inch	2
8-inch	$2\frac{1}{2}$
10-inch	3
12-inch	4
14-inch	5
16-inch	$6\frac{1}{2}$
heart-shaped	
9-inch	2
15-inch	4
oval	
6-inch	$1\frac{1}{2}$
13-inch	3

Royal Icing

Royal icing is the perfect medium for making flowers, bows, and delicate piped work. Extremely versatile, it is pure white and dries very hard. It will keep in an airtight container at room temperature for 2 weeks. Stir the icing to restore its original consistency after storage, but do not rebeat. Royal icing does not dry well in high humidity.

Yields 2½ cups

5 tablespoons meringue powder (found in cake-decorating stores)	OR 2 large egg whites, room temperature
3 ounces water	$\frac{1}{2}$ teaspoon cream of tartar
1 pound confectioners' sugar	2 teaspoons water
	1 pound confectioners' sugar

Combine all ingredients in a bowl and beat at slow speed with an electric mixer until the icing forms very stiff peaks and turns pure white. Add more sugar if the icing is not stiff enough, or a few drops of water if it is too stiff. Use immediately or cover the bowl with a damp cloth to prevent drying when not in use. Allow at least 24 hours for royal-icing decorations to dry at room temperature.

Servings

The following table lists how many servings you can expect from various sizes and shapes of cake pans, and how many cake recipes you will need for each. Most cake recipes yield approximately 6 cups of batter, enough to serve about 20 people. Each pan should be only half-filled with batter to ensure maximum baking efficiency. Serving sizes will vary depending on who is cutting the cake, but the amounts given are based on pieces about 3 to 4 inches high and 1 by 2 inches wide.

	pan	servings	
round or octagon	*square*		*heart-shaped*
6-inch 10	6-inch 15		6-inch 10
8-inch 20	8-inch 30		9-inch 20
10-inch 35	10-inch 50		12-inch 45
12-inch 50	12-inch 70		15-inch 70
14-inch 70	14-inch 100		
16-inch 100	16-inch 125		*hexagon*
18-inch 125			6-inch 12
	oval		9-inch 22
	6-inch 10		12-inch 48
	8-inch 30		15-inch 72
	10-inch 40		
	13-inch 70		

Basic Instructions

Building a Tiered Cake

A wedding cake must be very sturdy to stand throughout a long wedding without toppling when the happy couple finally cuts it. A multilayered wedding cake is actually a magnificent piece of engineering, made of graduated tiers of two or more layers with filling in between. The structure must be reinforced so that it does not collapse under the weight of the cake — cakes can be surprisingly heavy. The structure is only as strong as its foundation. Support is provided by $\frac{1}{4}$-inch-wide wooden dowels inserted into each tier, and in some cases all the way through the entire cake. Each tier rests on a separator board, which supports the cake on top of the dowels.

Separator boards should be the same size as the tiers they support. You can buy precut corrugated boards that match the size of most cake pans in cake-decorating stores, but I prefer to cut my own boards out of foamcore because it's sturdier and lightweight. Foamcore is available in most art-supply stores and cuts easily and cleanly with an X-acto knife.

To make boards, place the bottom of the pan in which your cake was baked on a piece of foamcore, trace the outline, and cut it out.

The cake layers for the tiers should be perfectly flat, but when they come out of the oven they usually are uneven. Wrap the cooled layers in plastic or foil and refrigerate for a few hours, then unwrap and level the tops with a large serrated knife. A chilled cake is easier to cut because it is firmer and less crumbly.

When you are ready to decorate the cake, decide how many layers of filling you want in each tier. For example, if you have 2 layers, each 2 inches high, you may want to slice each layer in half horizontally so that the final tier will consist of 3 layers of filling and 4 cake layers. Or you may keep each layer as is and have a tier of 2 layers with 1 layer of filling in between. If the layers are less than 2 inches high, 1 layer of filling should be enough.

Place the first layer right-side-up on the separator board. *Always use a dab of icing to hold a cake in place on the base or separator board, or when placing tiers on top of each other.* Then spread on the filling. If you are using a soft filling, such as jam, pipe a rim of buttercream icing around the outside edge before you add the filling, to keep it from oozing out. Add additional layers and filling. Place the top layer bottom side up. This gives a smooth and even surface on which to place the next tier, and also makes the cake look more professional.

If you are making a tier that is more than $4\frac{1}{2}$ inches high, place a separator board halfway between the 2 layers and insert dowels in the bottom half. Cover the top with buttercream and/or fondant before adding the second board. Then ice the entire tier to look like one layer (figure 1).

Place the tier on a turntable and fill in gaps between the layers with icing. To set the crumbs, spread a layer of thinned buttercream or ganache, using an angled spatula. This is known as crumb-coating. If you use

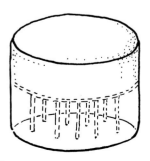

Figure 1

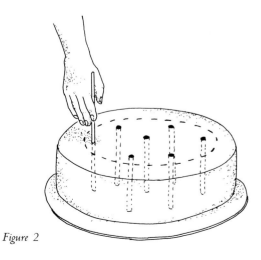

Figure 2

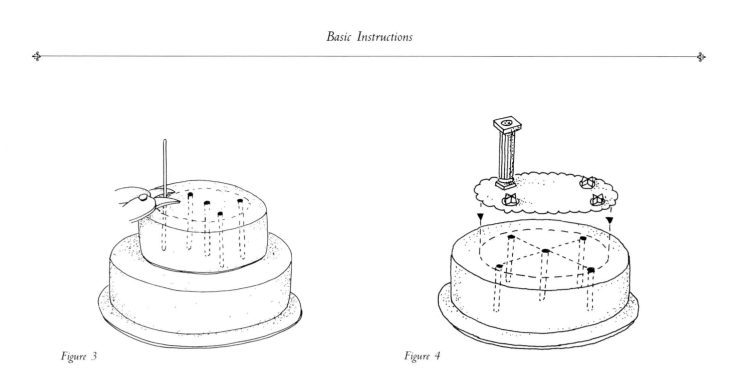

Figure 3   *Figure 4*

buttercream, the cake will need two or more coats to achieve a smooth finish. Let the first coat set before adding another. If you plan to cover the cake with rolled fondant, only one layer of crumb-coating is necessary, since that layer smooths the cake and helps the fondant adhere to the sides. *The directions for all of the cakes call for assembling the tiers on their corresponding foamcore boards. This includes filling and crumb-coating with the icing of your choice.*

When the buttercream icing is dry to the touch, or after you have covered the cake with fondant, place the cake pan for the next tier on the center of the larger tier. Lightly outline the pan with a toothpick. This gives you a perimeter in which to insert the dowels. Insert a dowel into the center of the tier until it touches the board. Using pruning shears, cut the dowel so that it is even with the top of the cake. Insert 6 more dowels around the inside of the outline and cut them as well (figure 2). Use fewer dowels for small tiers. The top tier doesn't need support unless you plan to add a heavy decoration. In that case, use 3 dowels in the top tier (figure 3).

If your cake is extremely tall or must be delivered in one piece, insert a dowel through the entire cake to reduce any swaying. Sharpen a dowel to a point and push it with a twisting motion through all of the tiers and the boards.

When a cake calls for columns between the tiers, substitute store-bought plastic separator plates for the foamcore boards. Such plates have pegs that hold the columns in place on both ends. A separator plate should be the same size or slightly larger than the cake it supports (figure 4).

Piping Techniques

Piping is the most creative part of cake decorating. Skilled piping transforms a simple cake into a masterpiece. Once you have mastered the basic techniques, you can combine them creatively and invent some of your own.

DOTS: Dots are made with a round tip that may vary in size from #00 to #12. Hold the tip at a 45-degree angle slightly above the cake and apply steady pressure to the pastry bag. Squeeze until the dot is the size you wish. Slowly pull the tip away from the dot with a slight swirling motion so that the dot is round, not pointed.

SNAIL TRAIL: A snail trail is a border made with a small, round tip. Hold the tip at a 45-degree angle against the cake, apply steady pressure, and let the icing build up slightly to form a dot. Then move the tip from left to right, stopping and starting at intervals to achieve a continuous dot-dash effect (figure 1).

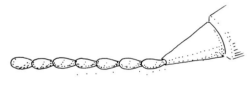

Figure 1

SHELLS: Shells are generally made with a star tip, most commonly sizes #13 to #32. Hold the tip at a 45-degree angle slightly above the cake. Apply steady pressure to the pastry bag and move the tip slightly away from you. As the icing starts to flow, lift the tip slightly. Relax the pressure and drag the tip down, ending in a point. Start the next shell on top of the point of the first shell (figure 2).

Figure 2

REVERSE SHELLS: Reverse shells are made in the same way as shells, but instead of having all of the shells face in one direction, you pipe one shell facing up and the next one facing down, and so on (figure 3).

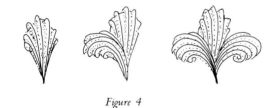

Figure 3

FLEURS-DE-LIS: Hold a star tip perpendicular to and slightly above the cake. Pipe a vertical shell that ends in a point (figure 4). Pipe another shell from left to right, to the left of and touching the first shell. Pipe a third shell from right to left, to the right of the first shell (figure 4).

Figure 4

ROPE BORDER: A rope can be piped using a star tip or a round tip. Hold the tip at a 45-degree angle and apply steady pressure. Pipe a continuous row of spirals with their sides touching (figure 5).

Figure 5

ROSETTES: Use star tips to make rosettes. Hold the tip at a 45-degree angle slightly above the cake. Apply steady pressure and move the tip in a full circle. Relax the pressure and break off the icing (figure 6).

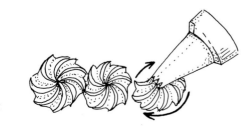

Figure 6

SCROLLS: Scrolls are generally made with a star tip. Hold the tip against the cake at a 90-degree angle, apply steady pressure, and move the tip in a circle. Go past the starting point, making a gentle downward curve (figure 7).

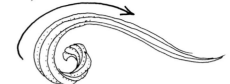

Figure 7

ZIGZAGS: Use a star or a round tip. Hold the tip at a 45-degree angle, slightly above the cake. Apply steady pressure and move the tip in a side-to-side motion. Each section should touch the one before it (figure 8).

Figure 8

BASKETWEAVE: You can use a ribbon, star, or round tip to make the vertical lines in a basketweave pattern. Use a ribbon tip (#46, #47, or #48) for the horizontal lines.

Place the tip against the cake at the top of the area to be decorated. Hold the tip perpendicular to the cake, apply steady pressure, and pipe a vertical line (figure 9). Pipe a horizontal band about $1\frac{1}{2}$ inches long from left to right across the top of the vertical line (the vertical line should be centered beneath). Leave a space below the band about the width of the ribbon tip. Pipe another horizontal band of the same length over the vertical line. Repeat down the length of the vertical line (figure 10).

Pipe a second vertical line on top of the right ends of the horizontal bands (figure 11).

Starting just at the right of the vertical line, pipe another row of horizontals bands, as above. Continue filling in the design (figure 12).

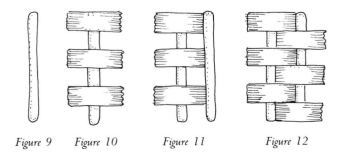

Figure 9   *Figure 10*   *Figure 11*   *Figure 12*

STRINGWORK: Pipe strings in royal icing only, using a round tip — usually #1, #1.5, or #2. I always use seamless tips, such as PME, to prevent the icing from spiraling out of the tip. Let the icing sit in a covered container for at least 24 hours before you use it; fresh icing has too many air bubbles and will cause the strings to keep breaking.

Practice this technique on a cake pan before you try it on a cake. Make evenly spaced marks around the cake, so you will know where the strings should begin and end. Place the tip against the cake at the first mark, hold the tip perpendicular to the cake, and apply pressure to the pastry bag. The icing will adhere to the cake. Slowly pull the tip away, continuing the pressure as the icing flows. Move the bag straight across to the next mark. Gravity will make the icing drop in an arc. Take your time and let enough icing flow to achieve the length you want and also to reach the next mark.

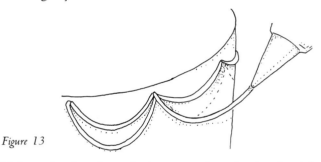

Figure 13

If the string breaks or is the wrong length, simply pick it up with a toothpick. It should come off the cake in one piece (figure 13).

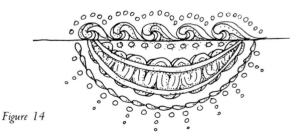

Figure 14

OVERPIPING: Overpiping simply means piping a design on top of another piped design to create a more elaborate and richly textured effect. For example, you might pipe a shell border using a star tip, then pipe strings over the shells with a small, round tip. Then you may want to pipe dots above the shells and add a rope border below. By combining simple techniques, you can turn a plain border into a spectacular one (figure 14).

Royal-Icing Flowers

Once you know the basic techniques, you can pipe almost any flower. Because royal icing dries relatively hard, icing flowers will last a long time if you keep them in a covered container at room temperature and don't expose them to humidity. The icing for piped flowers should be freshly made, because icing that's more than a day old tends to soften.

Flowers are often piped onto a flower nail or a sheet of wax paper. When they are dry, they can be placed directly on a cake. For bouquets, flowers are attached to a stem, while some types of flowers can be piped directly onto a stem.

A flower nail is a small, round, flat or cupped piece of plastic or metal on a stick. You hold it in one hand and turn it as you pipe with the other hand. Flower nails are a necessity for making most piped flowers.

The flat flower nail, which comes in various sizes, is used for making daisies, roses, chrysanthemums, carnations, and other flat-bottomed flowers (figure 1). I use the #7 (1½-inch) nail more than any other. For each flower, attach a 2-inch square of wax paper to the nail with a dab of icing and pipe the flower onto the paper. Remove the flower on the paper to dry.

The lily nail is cupped and comes in 4 sizes. You can use it to make morning glories, petunias, and other cupped flowers, as well as lilies (figure 2). Press a square of foil into the nail and fold it around the edges. Pipe the flower onto the foil and remove it on the foil to dry. Once the flower dries, it will come off the foil easily.

You can also make flowers on the flower nails using buttercream icing, but these cannot be stored for any length of time. But if you prefer soft flowers, use stiff buttercream icing and use only the flat flower nail. The buttercream cannot be removed from the foil if you use the lily nail.

To color flowers, tint the royal icing beforehand with paste food coloring. You can enhance the color by brushing the centers or edges of the petals with powdered food coloring to lend them a more realistic look. Brush powders only on flowers that are completely dry.

You can also paint a stripe of paste coloring inside the pastry bag before you fill it with icing. Place the stripe along the seam of the bag to keep track of where the color is. The icing will come out in a two-toned stripe, as striped toothpaste does. The flower will be darker on its outer edges or on the inside, depending on how you position the tip on the bag.

To create another striped effect, fill the pastry bag lengthwise with two different colors or shades of icing.

Flowers Made on the Flower Nail

The following directions list basic tip sizes. You can vary the size of the tip to make larger or smaller flowers.

BACHELOR'S BUTTON: Pipe a small mound of icing, using the #7 tip, on the wax paper on the flower nail. With the #65s leaf tip, pipe petals around the base of the mound (figure 3). Continuing to pipe petals, work your way up to the top of the mound to cover it completely (figure 4).

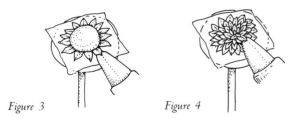

Figure 3   Figure 4

CHRYSANTHEMUM: Place a #80 or #81 tip halfway to the center of the nail on a 2-inch square of wax paper, keeping the round part of the tip against the paper. Pipe a petal out to the edge of the nail. Pipe a circle of petals around the nail (figure 5). Pipe another row of petals on top of the first row, starting them in slightly toward the center (figure 6). Add a third row of smaller petals on top of the second row.

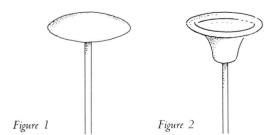

Figure 1   Figure 2

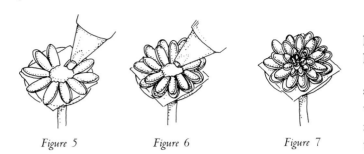

Figure 5	*Figure 6*	*Figure 7*

Finish the flower with very small petals in the center (figure 7).

DAISY: Place the wide end of the #104 rose tip at the center of the wax paper square and start piping, moving the tip out toward the edge of the paper and back toward the center again (figure 8). Begin and end each petal in the center. Turn the nail after you pipe each petal. Make 5 petals. Use the #5 tip to pipe a center (figure 9).

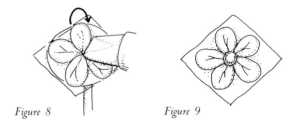

Figure 8	*Figure 9*

MARIGOLD: Tint the icing yellow-orange and add a burgundy stripe along the wide part of the tip, so that the inside of the petals is darker. Place the wide end of the #103 rose tip against the center of the wax paper. To pipe the first petal, move the tip straight out toward the edge, lift it slightly, and move it back to the center so that the end of the petal stands up (figure 10). Complete a circle of petals around the nail (figure 11). Pipe another shorter ring of petals on top of the previous ones. These petals should stand up a bit higher. Pipe another ring of shorter and more vertical petals to fill the top of the flower (figure 12).

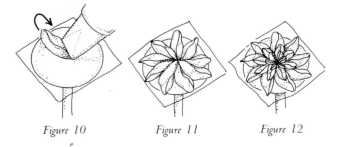

Figure 10	*Figure 11*	*Figure 12*

ROSE AND ROSEBUD: On a sheet of wax paper, pipe a large cone with the #9 tip. Let dry completely.

Use a dab of icing to place the cone on a 2-inch square of wax paper on a nail (figure 13). Place the wide end of the #104 tip at the base of the cone, narrow end facing up. Pipe around the cone, moving the tip up and then down while turning the nail counter-clockwise. Stop piping when you reach the beginning point.

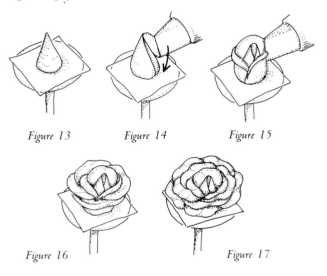

Figure 13	*Figure 14*	*Figure 15*

Figure 16	*Figure 17*

Pipe 3 petals around the bud, applying more pressure to the bag and holding the narrow end of the tip slightly away from the bud. Move the tip up, then down to form the petals (figure 14). You can stop here if you want a rosebud (figure 15). To make a full flower, add 4 larger petals, starting and ending at the center of the previous 3 petals (figure 16). Add 6 larger petals around the rose to finish (figure 17).

Flowers Made on the Lily Nail

ANEMONE: On the large lily nail, use the #126 rose tip to pipe a continuous band of icing inside the nail. The tip should be deep enough to fill in the center (figure 18). Insert a large stamen in the center, then many smaller stamens around it (figure 19).

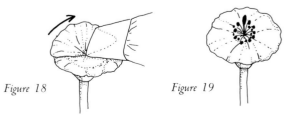

Figure 18	*Figure 19*

ASTER: Pipe many petals, using the #66 leaf tip (figure 20). Fill in the center with many stamens (figure 21).

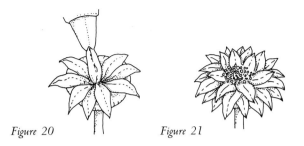

Figure 20   *Figure 21*

AZALEA: Place the #68 leaf tip in the center of the $1\frac{5}{8}$-inch nail. Pipe 5 evenly spaced petals, stopping just over the edge of the nail (figure 22). Insert 3 stamens (figure 23).

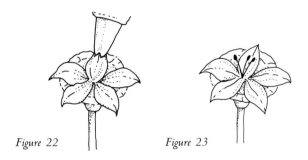

Figure 22   *Figure 23*

DAISY: Daisies have a cupped look when made on the lily nail. Place a square of foil in the nail but don't push it all the way to the bottom, so that it is shallower than the depth of the nail. Pipe a daisy as you would on a flat nail, using a rose tip (figure 24). Pipe a center with the #233 grass tip (figure 25).

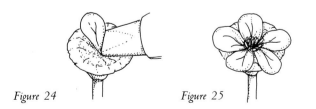

Figure 24   *Figure 25*

LILY: You can vary the type of lily by varying your piping speed. Piping faster creates smoother petals; piping more slowly gives the flower a ruffled look.

On the large lily nail, use the #70 leaf tip to pipe 3 evenly spaced petals out from the center of the nail (figure 26). Pipe 3 more petals in between the first 3

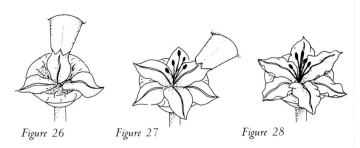

Figure 26   *Figure 27*   *Figure 28*

petals (figure 27). Insert 5 large stamens in the center (figure 28).

MORNING GLORY: Place the #126 rose tip, wide end down, in the center of the large nail. Pipe a continuous band of royal-blue or bright-magenta icing around the inside of the nail, ruffling the edge of the petal slightly. While you're piping, the tip should be deep enough to fill in the center of the flower (figure 29). Add 3 yellow stamens to the center. When the flower is dry, paint white stripes inside with liquid food coloring (figure 30).

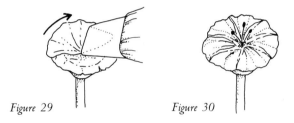

Figure 29   *Figure 30*

PETUNIA: Place the wide end of the #104 rose tip deep in the center of the nail. Pipe a petal out to the edge of the nail, then back to the center, as for making a daisy. As you pipe the petal, jiggle the tip

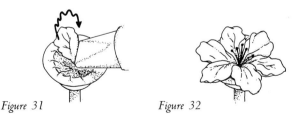

Figure 31   *Figure 32*

slightly to create a ruffled edge (figure 31). Pipe 6 petals. Insert 5 stamens (figure 32).

Flowers Made without a Nail

MULTI-PETALED DAISY: Another way to make a daisy is to pipe individual petals on a sheet of wax paper with a rose tip, holding the wide end of the tip away from you. Place the tip perpendicular to the paper and almost touching it when you begin to squeeze the pastry bag. Let the icing come out in a teardrop, then pull the bag toward you to lengthen it (figure 33). Stop piping when it comes to a point. Pipe about 20 petals for a large daisy and 12 to 15 for a small one.

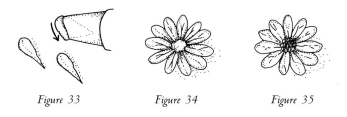

Figure 33   *Figure 34*   *Figure 35*

To assemble, pipe a mound of icing and insert the petals with the narrow end toward the center (figure 34). Pipe the center with the #233 grass tip (figure 35).

GRAPES: On wax paper, make grape clusters with the #4 round tip: Pipe a dot and let the icing drag to form a pointed tail. Pipe 2 more dots below the first (figure 36). Add 3 more dots (see figure 37). Pipe 2 more dots to finish (figure 38). To make larger clusters, use the #5 tip and add 5 more dots to the cluster.

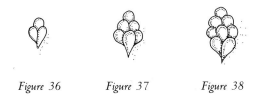

Figure 36   *Figure 37*   *Figure 38*

To make grapes on stems, insert the end of a 4- or 5-inch-long cloth-covered wire halfway into a finished cluster while the icing is wet. Let dry, then turn over and pipe grapes on the back.

CANTERBURY BELLS: Use stiff icing and the #16, #17, #18, or #19 star tip. Make sure that the points on the tip are all symmetrical, or the flower will be lopsided. Hold the tip perpendicular to and touch-

Figure 39   *Figure 40*   *Figure 41*

ing a sheet of wax paper. With the tip touching the paper *constantly*, apply pressure aggressively to the bag and the icing will eventually pop up to form a bell-shaped flower (figures 39–41).

LILACS: On wax paper, pipe pale purple icing into an elongated shell, using the #20 star tip (figure 42). Pipe darker purple blossoms on top of the mounds, using the #52 or #53 tip (figure 43).

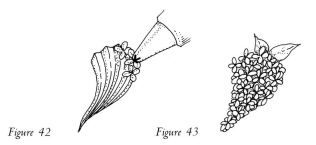

Figure 42   *Figure 43*

Flowers and Leaves Made Directly on Stems

Some flowers and leaves are piped directly on round toothpicks, bamboo skewers, or cloth-covered wires. Toothpicks and skewers should first be tinted green: Place them in a shallow dish and add green liquid food coloring and a few drops of water to cover the pieces. After a minute or so, place them on a bed of paper towels to dry.

Wrap cloth-covered wires with green florist's tape after the flower is dry.

HYACINTH: Insert a 4-inch green #22 wire into the #19 tip and 2 inches into a pastry bag that contains green icing. Apply pressure as you slowly pull the wire out of the tip (figure 44). The wire will emerge covered with rippled icing (figure 45). Insert this stem into a piece of Styrofoam to dry for 24 hours.

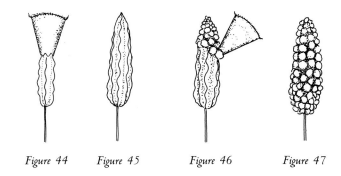

Figure 44   *Figure 45*   *Figure 46*   *Figure 47*

Fill another pastry bag with lavender icing and attach the #13 tip. Pipe puffs of lavender between the ridges of the green icing (figure 46). Cover the entire flower, then place the stem in Styrofoam to dry (figure 47).

ROSE and ROSEBUD: To make a rosebud, pipe icing directly on the end of a stem, as when using a nail, but continue past the starting point and go around twice. Place the stem in Styrofoam to dry. To make a rose, add petals around the bud, as described on page 151.

BABY'S BREATH: Insert a 3-inch #22 wire slightly into the #15 star tip on a pastry bag and pipe a white puff of icing on the end of each wire (figure 48).

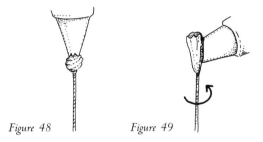

Figure 48   *Figure 49*

MORNING-GLORY BUD: Using the #104 rose tip with the narrow end facing up and the opening of the tip parallel to a #22 wire, pipe a tight ribbon of icing around the top of the wire. Allow the icing to fan out slightly at the top (figure 49). Brush the base of the bud smooth with a slightly damp paintbrush, if necessary.

LEAVES: Use toothpicks or bamboo skewers for stems. Cover a cookie sheet with wax paper. Insert one end of a stem about 1 to 1½ inches into the #5 round

tip, then apply pressure as you slowly pull it out. The coating of icing will help the leaf adhere to the stem (figure 50). Place the stem on the wax paper, where the wet icing will hold the stem in place while you pipe the leaf (figure 51). Place the end of the #114 large leaf tip, with the point facing down, on top of the coated stem and pipe out toward the end (figure 52). Extend the leaf about ½ inch beyond the end of the stem (figure 53). Let dry.

AUTUMN LEAVES: Tint icing various fall colors, including green. You can place them all in the same pastry bag to create multicolored leaves. You can also paint an orange, red, or purple stripe in the bag before adding green icing; the edge of the leaf will be striped with color, as if it's just starting to turn.

To make oak leaves, cover a stem with green icing as described above and place the stems on wax paper. Use the #104 rose tip to pipe daisy-petal shapes by moving the tip up and down along the stem (figure 54).

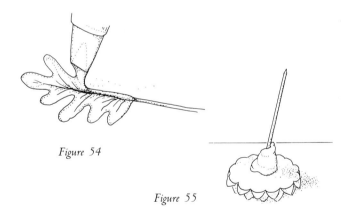

Figure 54

Figure 55

Placing Dry Icing Flowers on Stems

To attach a dry flower to a stem, remove the wax paper or foil from the flower and turn it upside down on a flat surface. Using the #7 tip, pipe a cone of stiff green royal icing in the center of the back of the flower. Insert a toothpick or skewer into the cone (figure 55). Let dry for 24 hours.

To make a bouquet or a vase of flowers, insert royal-icing flowers on stems into a Styrofoam ball. After the flower is in place, pipe icing from the #18 star tip onto the ball around the stem to hold the flower in place.

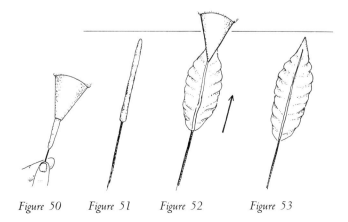

Figure 50   *Figure 51*   *Figure 52*   *Figure 53*

Gum-Paste Decorations

Gum paste is an edible material perfect for making highly realistic decorations. It can be rolled very thin and dries very hard with a porcelainlike finish. Gum-paste flowers seem to come alive when brushed with powdered colors. Although gum-paste decorations are fragile, they can be kept for years as mementos.

You can buy gum paste that is ready to use, such as Bakels, in cake-decorating stores. But it's almost as easy to make your own. Use a plastic, ceramic, glass, or stainless-steel bowl; other metal bowls may turn the paste gray. Mix Country Kitchen gum-paste powder with water, following the package directions. Add small amounts of the dry mix, if necessary, until the paste is no longer sticky. Shape the mixture into a ball and rub the surface with a little vegetable shortening. Place in a plastic bag, squeeze the air out, and seal. Store at room temperature in an airtight container for at least 24 hours to set. It will keep at room temperature indefinitely, but should be kneaded occasionally to restore its consistency.

Gum paste should snap when pulled apart. Knead in some of the gum-paste powder if it's too sticky, or some shortening if it's too dry.

Ribbons and Bows

Gum-paste bows have two components: loops and ribbon ends. These can be made on toothpicks, which are inserted into the cake, or without toothpicks and attached to the cake with icing. Either way, once you know the basic components, you can create various combinations.

Materials Needed:

cookie sheet
gum paste
plastic cutting board or rubber place mat
cornstarch
small plastic or wooden rolling pin

pizza cutter and small sharp knife
small dish of water
round toothpicks
small dish of vegetable shortening

Cover a cookie sheet with nontextured paper towels or tissue on which the ribbons can dry without sticking. Tint the gum paste, if desired, and knead thoroughly. Dust a cutting board or place mat with cornstarch.

To make a loop, roll out the gum paste about $\frac{1}{16}$ inch thick. Cut a 6-by-2-inch strip with a pizza cutter (this will make a medium-sized bow). Join the 2 ends and pinch together, making the end come to a point (figure 1). Stand the loop on its side to dry on the paper towels.

To make loops on toothpicks, roll out the paste and cut as above. Dip one end of a toothpick in water and fold both ends of the loop around it (figure 2). Set the loop on its side to dry.

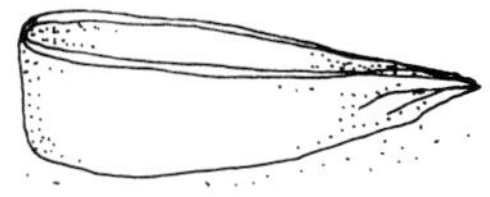

Figure 1

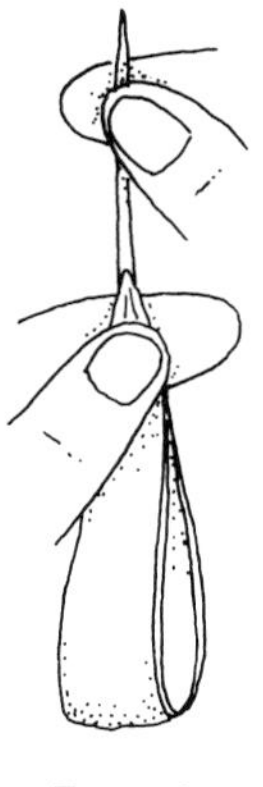

Figure 2

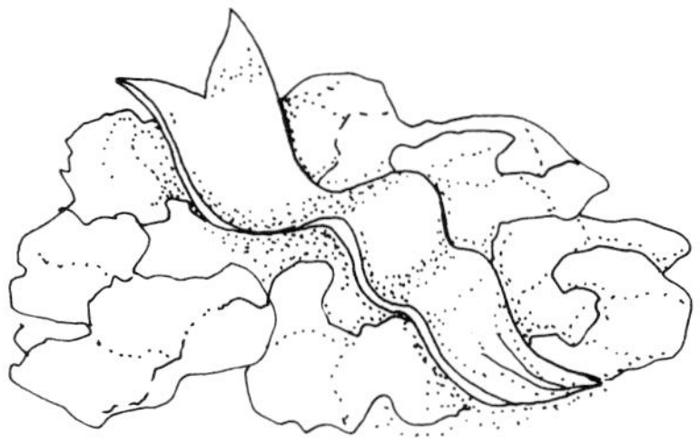

Figure 3

To make ribbon ends, cut a strip of gum paste the same width as the loops and whatever length you desire, depending on the design. Notch one end with a sharp knife. Pinch the other end so that it comes to a point. Prop the strip on crumpled tissue, to dry in a rippled formation (figure 3).

To make ribbons on toothpicks, cut strips with a pizza cutter to the desired width and notch one end. Dip one end of a toothpick in water and shake off the excess. Wrap the straight end of the ribbon around the damp end of the toothpick. Lay the strips out on the cookie sheet in a curved configuration.

Let the ribbons and loops dry for at least 2 days before you place on them on a cake. They can then be painted with powdered colors, if desired.

Flowers, Leaves, and Berries

To re-create these natural forms in gum paste, you need the following tools:

flower and leaf cutters
large and small ball tools
veining tool
trumpet-flower tool
leaf veiners
small rolling pin
plastic wrap
hard foam rubber
cornstarch
dish of water

small paintbrushes
heavy (#20 or #22), medium (#24), and lightweight (#26 or #28) cloth-covered wires
green and brown florist's tape
block of Styrofoam for drying
cookie sheets
powdered food coloring
paste food coloring
needlenose pliers

Roll out the gum paste on a smooth surface lightly dusted with cornstarch to avoid sticking. If you cut more petals or leaves than you can use immediately, cover the extra pieces with plastic wrap and then a damp cloth to prevent drying. Don't leave them for more than an hour or so, or they may become too dry to work with. Keep the gum paste wrapped in plastic while you work.

Roll the paste for petals very thin — it should be slightly translucent, so that you can almost read through it. Roll the paste thicker for leaves. Place the cutouts on a piece of hard foam rubber while you thin the edges of petals or work with various gum-paste tools. You can buy foam-rubber pads made for this purpose in cake-decorating stores.

Roll the ball tool around the edge of petals or leaves to thin the edges and make them curl. The harder you press, the more the petal will curl. Running the tool down the center of a petal makes the petal turn in on itself.

Figure 4

Trumpet-shaped flowers, such as daffodils, freesias, and morning glories, are all fashioned from one basic shape, which resembles a Mexican hat. Roll a small ball of gum paste into a pear shape and flatten the bottom with your fingers to form a brim (figure 4). Place the brim on the work surface and roll it very thin with a small rolling pin. Then follow the directions for each flower, given below.

While the cutouts are still soft, you can brush them with water to make them sticky to adhere to dried or soft gum paste. Dried paste will not stick with water, however; use royal icing.

Place the stem of the flower in a block of Styrofoam to dry. Always wrap florist's tape around the wire when you finish a flower.

Make pale-colored flowers and leaves in white gum paste. When dry, color them as needed: Brush powdered coloring on the entire flower, at the ends of the petals, or just in the center, using a soft, flat or pointed paintbrush. Dust green powder where the flower meets the stem and inside around the stamens. For dark flowers and green leaves, knead in paste or powdered coloring to soft gum paste. Flowers can also be painted with liquid colors to add intense dots or patterns.

APPLE BLOSSOM: Tape 5 stamens around a medium-gauge (#24) wire (figure 5). Shape a small Mexican hat. Roll the edges thin. Cut out a blossom (figure 6) and thin the edges with the ball tool (figure 7). Insert the ridged trumpet-flower tool and hollow and vein the center of the flower (figure 8). Dampen the center of the flower and insert the wire to just below the top of the tape. Press the bottom of the flower against the wire (figure 9).

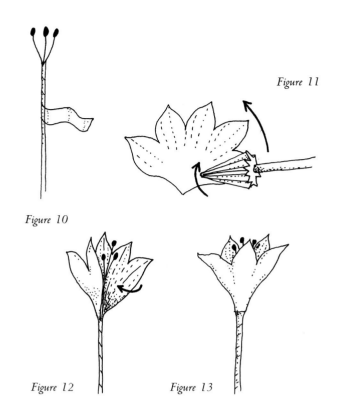

Figure 11

Figure 10

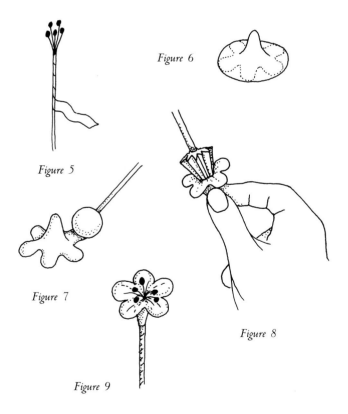

Figure 6

Figure 5

Figure 7

Figure 8

Figure 9

Figure 12

Figure 13

the flower and wrap it around the wire so that the tape does not show inside the flower. Press the two halves together (figures 12 and 13).

DAFFODIL: Tape 5 stamens onto a heavy-gauge (#20) wire (figure 14). Shape gum paste into a wide Mexican hat and roll the brim with a small rolling pin. Cut with a 6-petal cutter (figure 15). Insert the trum-

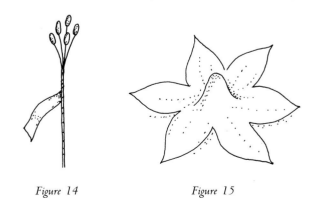

Figure 14

Figure 15

BELLFLOWER: Wrap 3 stamens around a medium-gauge (#24) wire with green florist's tape (figure 10). Roll out a piece of gum paste and cut out the flower. Emboss veins along the petals with the trumpet-flower tool (figure 11). Dampen the inside of

pet tool in the center of the flower to hollow it out and add veins to the center (figure 16). Using the veining tool, emboss veins from the center to the tips of the petals. Ruffle the edges of the petals slightly. Set aside, propped up with tissue.

Shape a piece of paste about $\frac{3}{4}$ inch long and $\frac{3}{8}$ inch thick into a Mexican hat. Using the ridged trumpet-flower tool, hollow out the inside to form a cup (figure 17). Use your fingers to pinch and thin the edges (figure 18). Place the cup on its side on a piece of hard foam rubber and ruffle the edge with a small ball tool (figure 19). Brush the bottom of the cup with a little water and attach it to the center of a flower. Brush the center with a little water and insert the end of the wire, stopping at the top of the tape (figure 20).

To make a daffodil without a wire, roll out gum paste and cut with the 6-petal cutter. Frill the edges

and emboss veins, as above. Let dry in a lily nail. Make the rest of the flower, as above, and let dry. Pipe royal icing into the center and insert 5 stamens.

DOGWOOD: Roll out a piece of gum paste and cut out the flower. Thin the petal edges with the ball tool. Using the veining tool, emboss veins in the petals, then gently press the veining tool in the indentation in the center of each petal (figure 21). Let dry on a slightly cupped foil square.

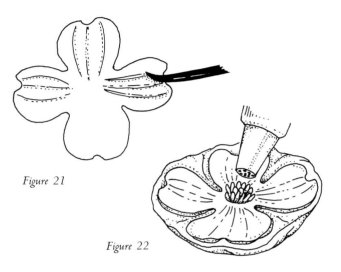

Figure 21

Figure 22

Pipe white royal-icing stamens in the center, using the #233 tip (figure 22). Let dry. Dust the center and the petal halfway up with pale-green powdered coloring. Using burgundy powder, dust the indentation in the center of each petal, brushing from the back toward the front.

FREESIA: Tape 4 yellow stamens to a fine-gauge (#26) wire (figure 23). Shape gum paste into a small Mexican hat and thin the edges with a small rolling pin. Cut out with a 6-petal cutter. Cut between each petal with an X-acto knife (figure 24). Insert the

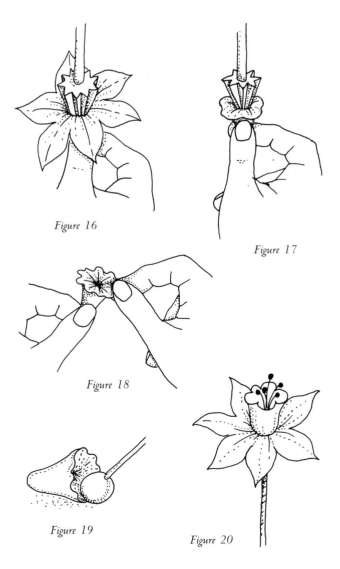

Figure 16

Figure 17

Figure 18

Figure 19

Figure 20

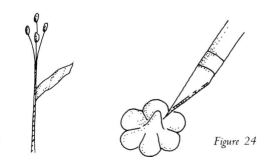

Figure 23

Figure 24

trumpet-flower tool into the center of the flower to hollow it out (figure 25). Cup and elongate each petal with the ball tool (figure 26).

Dampen the inside of the flower. Insert the wire with the stamens into the center, just to the top of the tape. Press the base of the flower tightly against the wire. Hang upside-down to dry if the petals start to droop.

To make buds, form a small amount of paste into a teardrop $\frac{1}{4}$ to $\frac{1}{2}$ inch long (figure 27). Insert a dampened wire into the paste, then mark one end with 4 even indentations, using an X-acto knife. Press the bottom of the bud tightly against the wire.

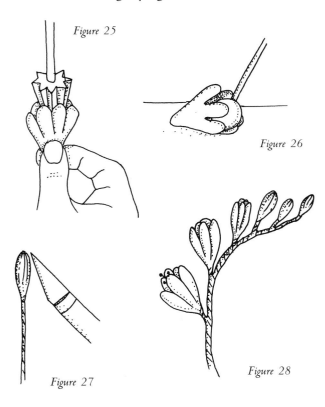

Figure 25

Figure 26

Figure 27

Figure 28

Dust the base of each blossom and bud with pale-green powdered coloring. Leave the flowers and buds white, or dust them with yellow, lavender, or pink powder. Tape the buds and flowers together: Start with the smallest buds on the end, add increasingly larger buds, and finally add flowers (figure 28).

LOTUS: Cut out one of each size flower. Using the large ball tool, elongate and curl each petal and press in the center to form a cup (figure 29). Dampen the inside of the larger flower and set the smaller one

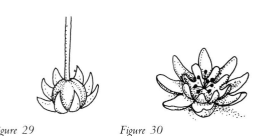

Figure 29   *Figure 30*

inside it. Press again in the center with the ball tool. Let dry on a cupped surface.

Pipe a dot of royal icing in the center, using the #3 tip. Insert many small stamens (figure 30). Let dry.

MIMOSA: Make a hook on the end of a medium-gauge (#24) wire. Attach a small ball of yellow gum paste onto the dampened, hooked end (figure 31). Let dry. Mix some cornmeal with a little yellow powdered coloring. Brush egg white on the paste, then sprinkle with cornmeal. Tape 3 to 6 stems together with green florist's tape (figure 32).

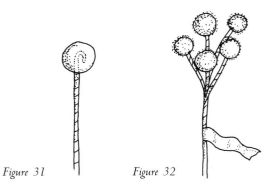

Figure 31   *Figure 32*

MORNING GLORY: Tape 3 yellow stamens to a medium-gauge (#22) wire (figure 33). Shape blue or magenta gum paste into a Mexican hat. Roll the brim very thin. Cut with a round cutter. Thin and ruffle the edges, using the large ball tool (figure 34). Insert the smooth trumpet-flower tool into the center to hollow it out (figure 35). With the veining tool, make 6 or 7 veins inside the flower (figure 36).

Dampen the inside of the flower. Insert the wire with stamens into the center, just to the top of the tape. Pinch the trumpet part of the flower and press it tightly against the wire (figure 37). Let dry. Paint white stripes inside the flower, using liquid coloring (figure 38).

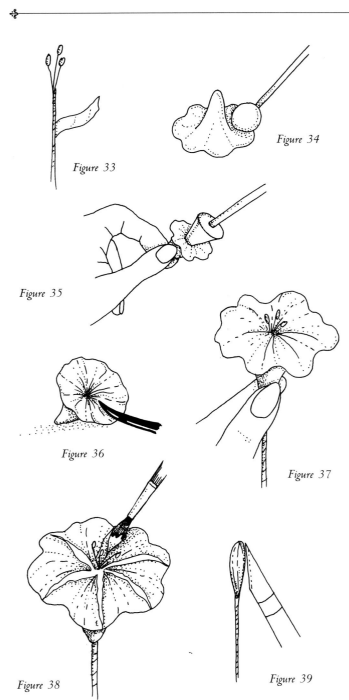

Figure 33

Figure 34

Figure 35

Figure 36

Figure 37

Figure 38

Figure 39

ball tool (figure 40). Brush water in the center of the circle and insert a #26 wire, to about $\frac{1}{2}$ inch from the top of the wire (figure 41). Press the circle all around the wire, fanning the top of the bud (figures 42 and 43).

Tape another wire and wrap it around a pencil to make curly trailers (figure 44). Tape the flowers, buds, and trailers together.

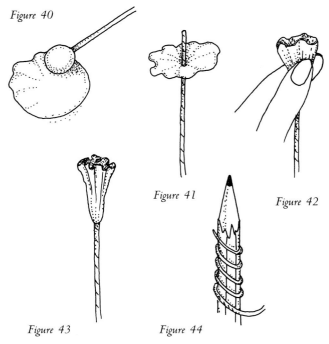

Figure 40

Figure 41

Figure 42

Figure 43

Figure 44

ORIENTAL PEONY: Tape 10 yellow stamens onto the end of a heavy-gauge (#20) wire and dampen the end (figure 45). Shape gum paste into a $\frac{3}{4}$-inch ball. Insert the wire into the ball, just to the top of the tape (figure 46).

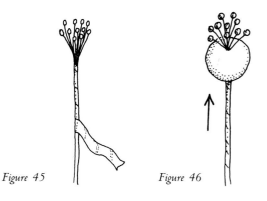

Figure 45

Figure 46

To make unopened buds, shape a piece of gum paste into a teardrop about $\frac{3}{4}$ inch long and $\frac{1}{4}$ inch thick. Brush the end of a fine-gauge (#26) wire with water and insert into the paste, pressing the end of the bud against the wire. Make 4 indentations with an X-acto knife in the thicker end (figure 39).

For a more mature bud, cut a circle of gum paste about 1 inch wide. Thin and ruffle the edges with the

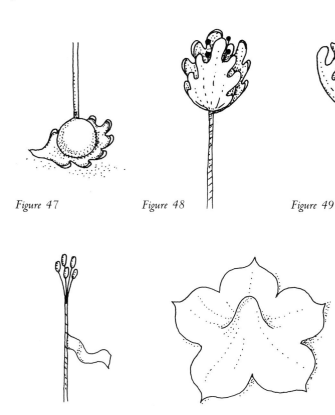

Figure 47 Figure 48 Figure 49 Figure 50

Figure 51 Figure 52 Figure 53

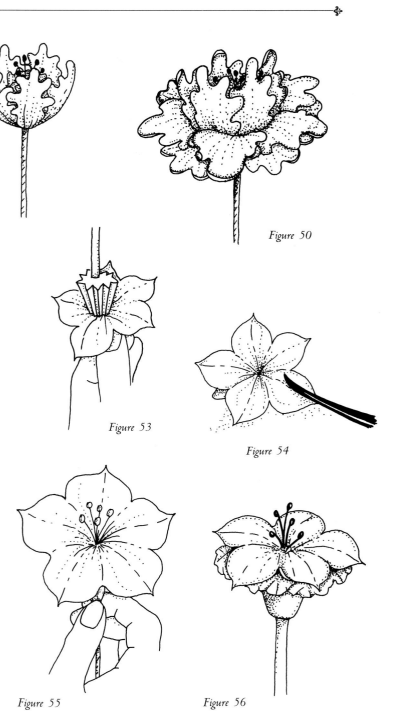

Figure 54

Figure 55 Figure 56

Cut out 3 petals with the smaller cutter. Thin the edges with the ball tool and curl the petals inward (figure 47). Brush a little water halfway up each petal. Attach the petals to the ball so that the top is even with the stamens and curls toward the center (figure 48). Let dry overnight.

Make 5 more petals. Attach to the flower, allowing the petals to fall away slightly from the center (figure 49). If the petals start to fall backward, make a hook in the end of the wire and hang the flower upside down to dry.

Add 7 larger petals, arranging them so that the tops curl outward. Dry on a bed of soft tissues to keep the petals from drooping (figure 50).

PETUNIAS: Tape 5 stamens onto a heavy-gauge (#20) wire (figure 51). Shape gum paste into a wide Mexican hat and roll the brim with a small rolling pin. Cut out flower (figure 52). Insert the trumpet-flower tool in the center to hollow it out and add veins (figure 53). On a piece of foam rubber, use the veining tool to emboss veins from the center to the tips of the petals and between each petal (figure 54). Ruffle the

petal edges. Brush the center with a little water and insert the end of the wire, stopping at the top of the tape. Press the trumpet around the wire (figure 55).

To make a petunia without a wire, roll out gum paste and cut. Vein the petals with the veiner and ruffle the edges. Let dry on a large lily nail (figure 56). Pipe royal icing in the center and insert stamens.

POPPY: Press a 3-inch square of foil onto a Styrofoam or plastic ball or egg. Cut 6 circles and ruffle the edges with the large ball tool. Pull one edge with the ball tool to elongate slightly (figure 57). Dampen the elongated edge of each petal and press the petals together in the center cup of the foil (figure 58). Let dry.

Shape a tiny ball of brown gum paste into a $\frac{3}{8}$-inch-long cone for the pistil. Using tweezers, pinch the wider end to form a star (figure 59). Brush the bottom with a little water and attach it to the center of the flower. Place many small black stamens around the pistil with a little black royal icing (figure 60).

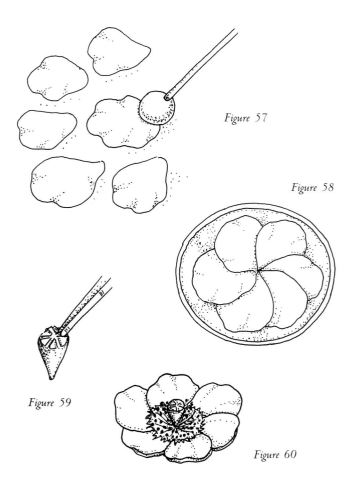

Figure 57

Figure 58

Figure 59

Figure 60

PRIMULA: Tape 3 stamens around a medium-gauge (#24) wire (figure 61). Shape a small Mexican hat and roll the edges thin. Cut out the larger blossom. Thin the edges with the ball tool (figure 62).

Cut out a small petal with the other cutter. Brush a little water inside the first blossom and attach the

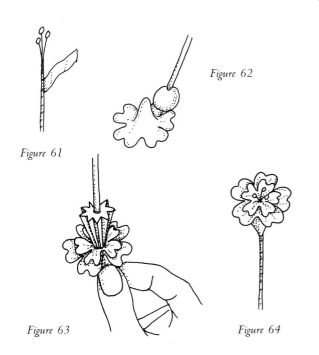

Figure 61

Figure 62

Figure 63

Figure 64

small blossom to it. Insert the ridged trumpet-flower tool and hollow and vein the center of the flower (figure 63).

Dampen the center of the flower and insert the wire to just below the top of the tape. Press the bottom of the flower against the wire (figure 64).

RASPBERRIES: Make a tiny hook on the end of a medium-gauge (#24) wire and dampen slightly. Insert a small ball of dark red gum paste on the hook (figure 65). Let dry.

Pipe small dots on the ball, using red royal icing and the #2 tip, starting at the end farthest from the wire. Let dry (figure 66). Brush with egg white to create a sheen. Pipe a calyx with the #65S tip in green royal icing (figure 67). Tape 2 or 3 stems together with green florist's tape.

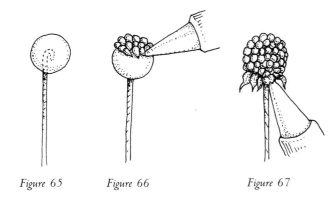

Figure 65   *Figure 66*   *Figure 67*

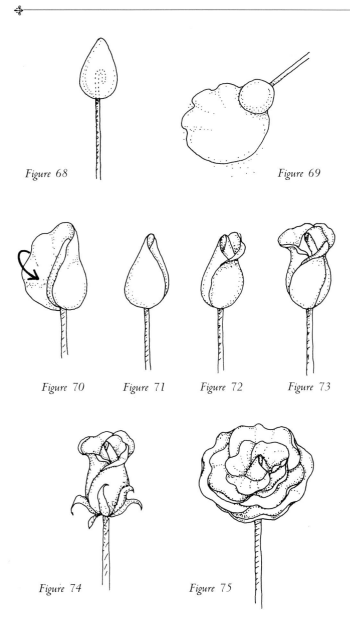

Figure 68

Figure 69

Figure 70   Figure 71   Figure 72   Figure 73

Figure 74   Figure 75

Make three petals, using the #1 cutter. Thin the edges and attach them to the bud, overlapping and evenly spaced (figure 72). Curl and pinch the tips backward slightly (figure 73). Cut a calyx from green gum paste. Thin and elongate the petals with the ball tool. Brush the calyx with water and insert the wire through to the bud. Press against the bud and allow the tips to curl down (figure 74).

To make a full rose, don't add the calyx, but do add 5 more petals, using the #2 (I¼-inch) cutter. If the petals start to sag, hang them upside down by the wires until they hold their shape.

For an even fuller rose, add 6 or more petals from the #3 (I½-inch) cutter (figure 75).

SMALL 2-PIECE ROSE ON TOOTHPICK:
Cut a small circle of gum paste and thin the edges slightly. Dampen the circle and wrap it around the end of a toothpick (figures 76 and 77).

Cut a 5-petal blossom and thin the edges. Brush the inside with a little water. Push the end of the toothpick into the center and push the blossom up to meet the wrapped circle (figure 78). Press the petals, overlapping, around the inside of the flower. Fold back the tops of the petals, as on a regular rose (figure 79). To make a larger rose, attach another 5 petals below. Let set until the petals are stable, then carefully slide the flower off the toothpick to dry completely (figure 80).

ROSE AND ROSEBUD: Shape a small ball of gum paste into a cone (the size of the cone will determine the size of the rose). For a small rose, use a ball about ⅜ inch in diameter; for a large rose, use a ball at least ½ inch in diameter. Make a tiny hook on the end of a heavy-gauge (#20) wire and dampen slightly. Insert the wide end of the cone halfway onto the hook (figure 68). Let dry overnight.

Roll out a thin piece of gum paste and cut a circle with the #1 (I-inch) circle cutter. Thin the edges with the large ball tool (figure 69). Dampen the inside of the circle slightly and wrap around the cone to form the inside of the rose (figures 70 and 71).

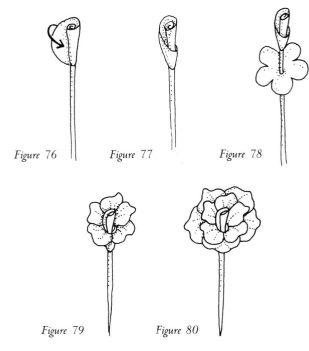

Figure 76   Figure 77   Figure 78

Figure 79   Figure 80

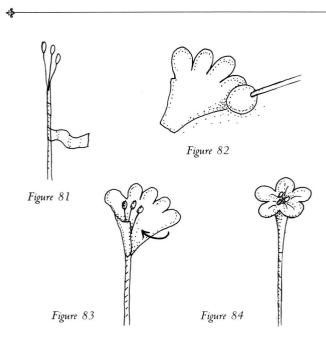

Figure 81

Figure 82

Figure 83

Figure 84

Make 25 petals out of yellow-orange gum paste, using the small ($\frac{3}{4}$-inch) rose-petal cutter. Vein each petal with the straight leaf veiner (figure 86). Dry the petals on a curved surface (figure 87). Let dry overnight.

Remove the cones from the wax paper and place the stems in a piece of Styrofoam to keep them upright while you apply the petals. Tint some royal icing to yellow-orange to match the petals. Attach a row of petals around the edge of the cone with dots of icing, using the #2 tip. Add another row of petals on top, overlapping the first row (figure 88).

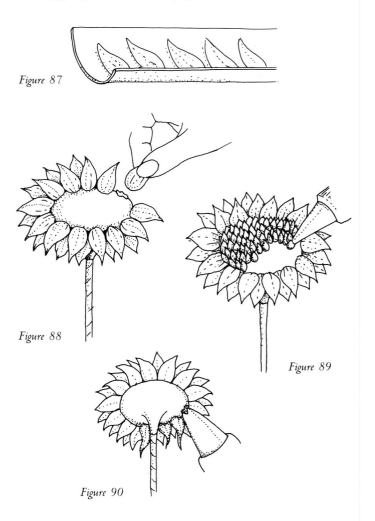

Figure 87

Figure 88

Figure 89

Figure 90

STEPHANOTIS: Wrap 3 stamens around the end of a medium-gauge (#24) wire (figure 81). Cut a white blossom. Elongate and thin the petals and the extended edge with the ball tool (figure 82). Place the wire on the side opposite the extended edge. Wrap the flower around the wire so that the petals meet at the extension (figure 83). Smooth the seam. Bend the petals back away from the center (figure 84).

SUNFLOWER: Wrap 4 heavy-gauge (#20) wires, 6 inches long, together with green florist's tape. On a piece of wax paper, pipe a large cone of stiff royal icing, about $1\frac{1}{2}$ inches wide at the base and $1\frac{1}{4}$ inches high, using the #10 tip. Insert one of the taped wires upright into the icing and let dry overnight (figure 85).

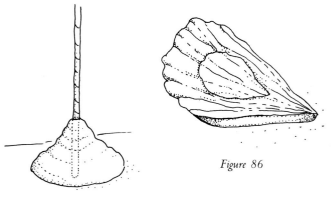

Figure 86

Figure 85

Using brown icing, pipe dots from the #3 tip all around the inside (the flat part) of the flower (figure 89). Tint some royal icing moss-green and pipe calyxes underneath the flower with the #67 leaf tip, covering the cone of royal icing (figure 90).

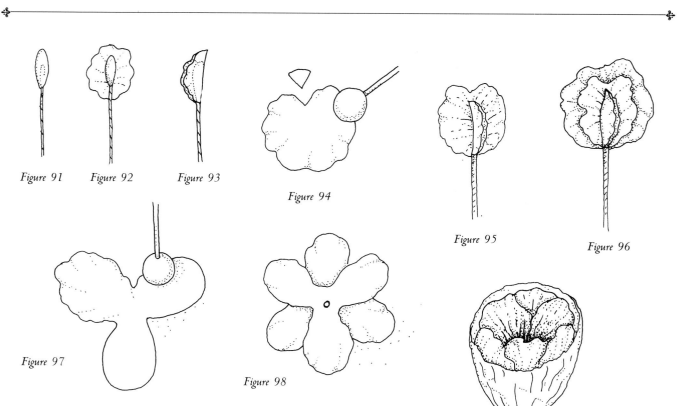

Figure 91 *Figure 92* *Figure 93*

Figure 94

Figure 95

Figure 96

Figure 97

Figure 98

Figure 99

SWEET PEA: Make a small hook at the end of a piece of medium-gauge (#24) wire, 3 inches long. Dampen slightly. Shape a small pea of gum paste about $\frac{3}{8}$ inch long and insert it on the hook (figure 91).

Cut a 1-inch circle of gum paste. Thin and slightly ruffle the edges with the ball tool. Dampen the inside of the circle and place the pea in the center (figure 92). Fold the circle in half so that the fold faces forward. Leave the edges a bit open (figure 93).

Cut another circle with the $1\frac{1}{4}$-inch cutter and cut a small V out of the top edge. Ruffle the edges and dampen the inside (figure 94). Place the folded edge of the covered pea inside the circle so that the V is at the top. Pinch the pea and petal together (figure 95).

Cut a third petal with the $1\frac{1}{2}$-inch circle cutter. Thin and ruffle the edges and dampen the inside. Place the flower inside this petal and pinch gently. The third petal should be more open than the preceding one (figure 96).

TULIP: Form a 5-inch square of foil into a cup on the end of a plastic egg. Roll some gum paste very thin and cut 2 sets of 3 petals. Thin the edges with the large ball tool (figure 97).

Brush a little water in the center of one set of petals and place the other 3 petals on top and in between the

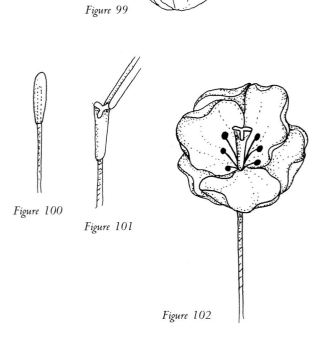

Figure 100

Figure 101

Figure 102

first set. Press the centers together (figure 98). Place the flower inside the foil cup, making sure that all of the petals are upright (figure 99). Poke a hole through the bottom of both layers of petals and the foil. Let dry.

To form the pistil, shape a small piece of yellow gum paste into a sausage about $\frac{1}{2}$ x $\frac{3}{16}$ inch. Dampen the end of a 3-inch length of heavy-gauge (#20) wire and insert it into the end of the pistil, stopping before it comes through the other end (figure 100). Use tweezers to pinch the end three times (figure 101). Remove the foil from the tulip. Brush the bottom of the pistil with a little water and insert it into the hole in the flower. Place the flower on a rack so that the wire hangs down. Let dry.

Pipe some yellow royal icing around the base of the pistil, using a small tip, and insert 6 black stamens in the icing around the pistil (figure 102).

TINY BLOSSOMS: Cut out blossoms and press the centers with the small ball tool to form a cup (figure 103). Let dry. Pipe a #2 dot of royal icing in the center. To place the flowers on stems, pipe a little royal icing on the end of a fine-gauge (#28) wire. Place the flower on the icing and let dry (figure 104).

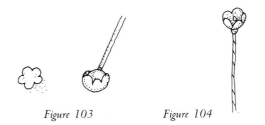

Figure 103   *Figure 104*

BUDS: Make a tiny hook on the end of a piece of fine-gauge (#28) wire. Shape a small piece of gum paste into a tiny ball about $\frac{3}{8}$ inch wide. Brush the hooked end of the wire with a little water and insert into the ball of paste (figure 105). Let dry. These can be taped together and to the blossoms (figure 106).

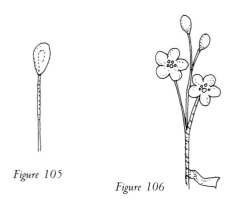

Figure 105

Figure 106

LEAVES: To make leaves without wires, simply cut the leaves and vein them with a leaf veiner. Place them on a bed of crumpled paper towels to dry.

To make leaves on wires, roll out a piece of gum paste so that one end is thicker than the other. Cut out a leaf with the bottom at the thicker end (figure 107).

Dampen the end of an appropriate-sized hooked wire and insert the wire into the end of the leaf, pushing it in $\frac{1}{4}$ inch at the most (figure 108). Press the paste around the wire to secure. Vein the leaf. Let dry on crumpled tissues.

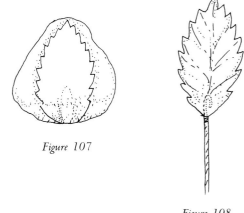

Figure 107

Figure 108

FABRIC ROSE: Cut a 3-by-1-inch strip of gum paste and roll it to the desired size of the flower (figure 109). With your fingertips, squeeze one end of the roll together and fan out the other end to form a rose (figure 110).

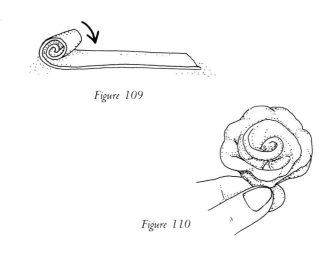

Figure 109

Figure 110

Gum-Paste Cutters

Cake-decorating stores sell gum-paste cutters in these shapes for the various cakes in this book. They can be purchased from many of the sources listed on page 182.

Art Deco Cake

Art Deco Cake —
Pineapple Leaves

Art Deco Cake
Chocolate Fantasia

Chocolate Fantasia
Chocolate Groom's Cake
Strawberry Cake

Art Deco Cake

Art Deco Cake

Tiny Blossom

Sunflower Petal

Sunflower Petal

Sunflower Petal

Edwardian Cake

Birch-Bark Cake

Stephanotis

Chocolate Fantasia

Oriental Apple Blossom Cake

Bellflower
Art Deco Cake

Lotus

Lotus

Strawberry Cake

Strawberry Cake

Tulip
Chocolate Fantasia

Apple Blossom
3-Piece Rose

Strawberry Cake

Fabergé Topiary

Chocolate Fantasia

Apple Blossom
3-Piece Rose
Daffodil
Freesia

Primula

Primula

Primula

Dogwood

Majolica Cake

Petunia
Chocolate Fantasia

Oriental Peony

Oriental Peony

Blue Delftware

Leaves

Daffodil

Leaves

Leaves

Rose
Morning Glory
Sweet Pea
Poppy

3-Piece Rose
Chocolate Fantasia

Leaves

Leaves

Leaves

Sweet Pea
Morning Glory
Rose
Poppy

Rose
Morning Glory
Sweet Pea

Rose

Run-in Sugar

Run-in sugar is a technique in which thinned royal icing is flooded into a preoutlined shape on wax paper. You can use it to make decorations on wires, toothpicks, or bamboo skewers simply by laying the wire or skewer in the center of the design before you fill it in. The dried icing will hold the wire or skewer tightly in place after you fill in the back of the design, as well. This also makes a design that can be seen from 2 sides.

To make a run-in sugar design, place the pattern you want to reproduce on a flat surface and tape a piece of wax paper on top. Outline the design with stiff royal icing, using the #2 tip for small or intricate patterns and the #3 tip for larger designs. Place some stiff royal icing in a bowl and stir in a few drops of water. Continue adding water, a few drops at a time, until the icing has the consistency of corn syrup and a teaspoonful dropped into the bowl disappears by the count of 10. Pipe the icing into the outlined design with the #2 tip, filling in the entire shape up to the outline (figure 1).

Depending on the size of the design and the humidity in the air, let the decoration dry for at least 24 hours. Use a metal spatula or a palette knife to remove it from the wax paper. (*Hint:* When using two or more colors in a run-in design, let the first color dry before you add the second color. This will prevent the colors from bleeding into one another.)

Figure 1

Sugar Molds

Molding a form in sugar is an easy way to make an edible vase to hold edible flowers on top of a cake. You can use any metal, plastic, or glass cup, bowl, tart tin, or measuring cup with a smooth surface as a mold. You probably already have many containers that will work quite well. (Of course, the top of the form must be larger than the bottom, or the mold won't come out.) Sugar molds dry very hard, and they can be hollowed out before they are completely dry to make them more lightweight.

To make a sugar mold, place 1 cup of granulated sugar in a bowl and add 1 tablespoon of cold water. If you want to make a colored mold, add some food coloring to the water and mix thoroughly before adding it to the sugar. The colored water will appear darker before you mix it with the sugar, so tint the water a little darker than you want it to be. Mix the sugar with your hand until all of the sugar is damp. Using your hand is messy, but it makes it easier to tell when the sugar is thoroughly mixed.

Pack the sugar tightly into a clean container, pressing the sugar into the mold firmly with your hand. Level off the top with a knife and invert the sugar onto a piece of wax paper. Gently lift off the container. If the sugar doesn't come out easily, pick it up and turn it over again, tapping the container. Let the sugar dry overnight, upside-down. Do not disturb the mold, or it will crumble.

After the sugar has set but is not completely dry, hollow it out by carefully turning it right-side-up and scooping out the damp sugar with a spoon. Be careful not to make the sides of the mold too thin. Then let the mold dry completely, right-side-up, for 24 hours.

You can attach a Styrofoam ball or egg in the hollow part of the mold with royal icing and then insert sugar flowers into the Styrofoam. If you like, decorate the outside of the mold with royal icing, gum paste, or rolled fondant.

Quilting

Quilting is a technique I developed years ago, based on bedspread patterns and quilted bags. I realized that I could achieve this look on rolled fondant by using a tracing wheel with little pointed teeth. The teeth emboss small holes in the icing in straight or curved lines to simulate sewing stitches.

Tiers must be quilted before they are stacked, and the quilting should be done immediately after you apply the fondant. Once the fondant starts to dry, the quilting may not show up.

On a square or rectangular cake, always start on the top, then use those lines as a guide to quilt the sides. A cake of any other shape *must be quilted on the sides first.*

Equipment needed:

tracing wheel
triangle (30-60-90-degree or isosceles right)
18-inch metal ruler

To quilt a square or rectangular cake:

Cover the cake with rolled fondant and place the cake on a board. Then set the tier on a turntable, which makes it much easier to work on all sides. Use a ruler that is long enough to reach both corners when placed on the cake diagonally. The width of the ruler will determine the size of the quilt squares, so pick a size that suits the size of the cake. To decorate a 6-inch cake, for example, choose a ruler about I inch wide. For a larger cake, use a wider ruler.

Place the ruler diagonally on top of the cake so that it touches two opposite corners. Run the tracing wheel along both sides of the ruler to emboss two dotted lines. Move the ruler over against one of the dotted lines and emboss another line on the other side of the ruler. Cover the top of the cake with diagonal lines going in one direction, then turn the cake and repeat in the opposite direction.

To quilt the sides of the cake, align one edge of a triangle with the lines at the top edge of the cake.

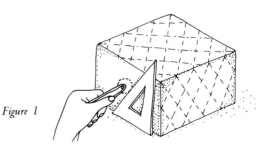

Figure 1

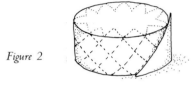

Figure 2

Emboss lines along the angled edge of the triangle. Turn the triangle and emboss lines in the other direction (figure I).

To quilt an octagonal cake:

Only the sides are quilted, one section at a time. Measure out the divisions, then use the same technique as for the side of a square cake.

To quilt a round or heart-shaped cake:

Cover the cake with fondant. Wrap a tape measure around the circumference. Decide approximately how big you want the design to be — for example, 2 inches. The distance between the lines must divide evenly into the circumference. Mark the cake around the base with a toothpick at these divisions. Trace a triangle out of flexible cardboard, so that it can bend to follow the contour of the sides of the cake. Place the bottom of the triangle at each mark and emboss diagonal lines on the sides, as above.

To emboss the top of the cake, continue the lines from the sides of the cake onto the top. You will end up with a star pattern rather than a grid (figure 2).

Painting with Gold and Iridescent Colors

To color gum paste, rolled fondant, or royal icing with gold, silver, or another nontoxic iridescent colored powder, use lemon extract to make the "paint." The high percentage of alcohol and the lemon oil in the extract makes the paint spread smoothly and dry quickly, before the icing gets soggy. It can be found in the grocery store.

Mix a little powdered coloring with a few drops of extract and stir with a small brush. To check the consistency, paint some spare fondant. If the color streaks, add a little more powder; if it's too thick, add more extract. The alcohol in the extract will evaporate, so you may need to add more extract while you work.

When you finish, set the container aside and let the mixture dry out. You can reuse it simply by adding more extract.

Octagonal Cakes

Since there are no 8-sided cake pans, you need to cut a cake made in a round pan into an octagon. To make a template for this shape, outline the bottom of a pan on a sheet of paper and cut it out. Fold the paper circle in half, then into quarters, then into eighths. Place a ruler across the 2 points that form the ends of the arc (figure 1), draw a line, and cut off the rounded part. When you open the paper, you will have an octagon. Place the pattern flat on a foamcore board, outline it, and cut it out with an X-acto knife. This foamcore octagon will be the base for the tier.

After stacking the cake layers into a tier, place the paper pattern on top and cut the cake vertically to form an octagon. Secure the tier on the base with a dab of icing.

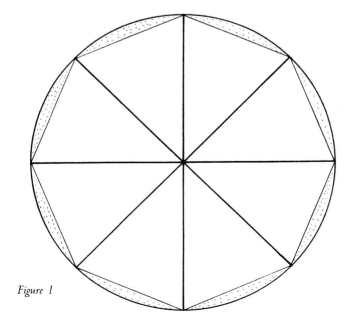

Figure 1

Marking Divisions on a Cake

To decorate a cake with a regular pattern on the sides or the top, you need guidelines for piping. Your cake will have a much more professional look if the decorations are evenly spaced. The following techniques work for circular, square, and rectangular cakes. For other shapes, such as ovals and hearts, use a tape measure to divide the cake into equal sections.

A simple way to find the center of a cake is with a piece of paper cut to the size of the cake. Trace the bottom of the pan in which the cake was baked on a piece of paper and cut it out. Fold the paper in half, then into quarters. Open the paper and make a small hole in the center with a toothpick. Place the paper on the top of the cake and mark the center with a toothpick.

To divide a cake, fold the paper into quarters as above, then once more into eighths or twice more into sixteenths (figure 1). Open the paper, place it on the cake, and mark with a toothpick at each fold.

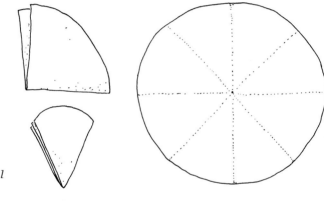

Figure 1

Cake Bases

The base for a wedding cake must be strong enough to support its weight and attractive enough to enhance its beauty. Depending on the cake, the base should be *at least* 2 inches larger than the bottom tier. (This leaves only 1 inch from the cake to the edge all around.) If you plan to put flowers or other decorations around the bottom edge, make sure the base is large enough to accommodate them.

Bases can be made from many materials, such as plywood, masonite, foamcore, plastic, or fiberboard. Plywood, masonite, or plastic are strong but also heavy and difficult to cut into circles or odd shapes. Plastic can be very expensive. I find that ready-made, $\frac{1}{2}$-inch-thick fiberboard bases with a foil wrapping are the strongest and lightest. These bases are available at cake-decorating stores and come in the same sizes and shapes as most cake pans, up to 24 inches wide. You can cover the foil wrapping with thinned royal icing or rolled fondant to match the cake.

You can make your own bases by assembling layers of foamcore cut with an X-acto knife to the shape and size of the cake. Foamcore should not be used for cakes larger than 16 inches, though, because it may bend. If a base bends when you lift it, it can crack the cake. Two layers of $\frac{1}{4}$-inch foamcore glued together should be strong enough to hold most 1- or 2-tiered cakes. The wider the base of the cake, the thicker the board should be.

To make a base from foamcore, trace the outline of the shape you want on the boards and cut out with a sharp X-acto knife. Glue the boards together with white glue and place some heavy books on top so they dry flat. Use a third layer if the cake is very big or heavy.

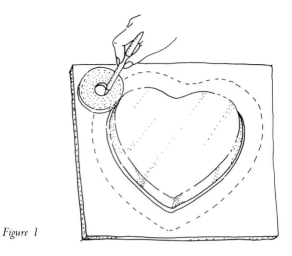

Figure 1

To make a base for an irregularly shaped cake, such as a heart or oval, use the cake pan as a template to enlarge its outline. Set the pan used for the bottom tier on a large piece of foamcore. To make a 19-inch base for a 15-inch cake, for example, you need to measure 2 inches of foamcore all around the pan. To do so, use a roll of tape that measures 2 inches from the inner surface to the outer surface (figure 1). Place the outside of the roll against the pan and insert a pen or marker in the hole. Roll the tape along the edge of the pan, marking the board as you roll. You will end up with a perfectly enlarged shape drawn on the board.

Covering the base with thinned royal icing is the easiest and most lightweight way to make the board attractive. Thin enough icing to cover the board by adding a few drops of water at a time until the icing is the consistency of thick syrup. Tint the icing to match a colored cake, if desired, or leave it white. Pour it onto the board and smooth with a spatula. Set aside to dry for at least 24 hours.

To cover the edge of the board, glue a ribbon around it with white glue. The ribbon should be the same height as the board. This gives the cake a very elegant and professional look.

Use a dab of royal icing to secure the cake to the base and keep it from shifting if you have to move it.

Styrofoam

Styrofoam may seem like an unusual material to use for creating wedding cakes, but it has many uses for decorating and often forms the structure of a cake. It comes in 2 types: one has a dense, coarse texture, and the other is softer, more flexible, and breaks off into small beads. Styrofoam comes in many sizes and shapes, such as disks, sheets, eggs, and balls, and can be found at craft, art-supply, and cake-decorating stores. It's easy to cut and shape, and is both lightweight and strong.

You can buy sheets of Styrofoam as thin as $\frac{1}{2}$ inch or as thick as 4 or 5 inches. When making stemmed flowers, I always have a 2-inch-thick sheet of Styrofoam nearby to stick the stems in while I work. The flowers dry upright, without becoming crushed or misshapen from lying on their sides. Transporting flowers in Styrofoam is also a handy way to avoid breakage.

Styrofoam balls or eggs are useful for making bouquets of flowers and bows. They can hold flowers in sugar vases (page 170) or, when cut in half, support arrangements on top of a cake or in the center of a separator plate.

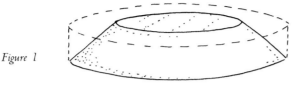

Figure 1

(A ball or egg is glued into a sugar mold or onto a separator plate with royal icing, and when the icing is dry, the stems are inserted into the Styrofoam. Royal icing is then piped around the stems to hold them in place.)

When placing a half-ball of Styrofoam on top of a cake, first cover the cut side of the ball with aluminum foil so that any stray flakes of Styrofoam won't fall into the icing. Simply cut a piece of foil about an inch larger all around than the bottom of the ball. Place the ball in the middle of the foil and fold up the sides. The foil won't show when it's covered with royal icing.

Styrofoam disks can be purchased in the same sizes as cake layers. Generally used for making cakes for display purposes, they are covered with icing and decorated in the same way as actual cakes. It's easier to use Styrofoam than real cake for making beveled layers because cake tends to fall apart at the thin edge. A Styrofoam bevel is also a strong support for other layers.

To cut and shape Styrofoam, use a serrated knife, such as a steak knife. Use a sawing motion, as if you were cutting bread. Cut the Styrofoam roughly, then sand it with a piece of the coarser type of Styrofoam until smooth and the size and shape you want. Try to work outdoors or over a trash can when sanding and cutting Styrofoam, because it generates a lot of little shavings that will stick to everything in the room, including you.

To make a beveled layer, start with a disk that is the proper height and diameter for your cake. For example, if you choose a 10-inch disk and you want to place an 8-inch tier on top, you must cut the disk so that the top of the bevel measures 8 inches. Center the bottom of an 8-inch cake pan on the disk and trace its outline with a marking pen (figure 1). Cut diagonally from the base to the outline. Sand the cut edge with another piece of Styrofoam until it is smooth and even. After you cover the cut edge with icing, the beveled layer will be indistinguishable from the rest of the cake.

Transporting Wedding Cakes

If your cake must travel even a short distance, make sure that it's sturdy enough to withstand the trip. Most wedding cakes are very heavy and tall, so I don't recommend delivering them in one piece unless absolutely necessary. The entire cake may be difficult to lift and could tip over as your vehicle turns a corner. Transport each tier separately, in its own box, and assemble the cake when you arrive at your destination — especially if there are any columns on the cake. Place the boxes on top of a piece of foam rubber to cushion the bumps. Any top decorations, such as a vase of flowers, should also be added after arrival. Bring along some extra icing to add borders and do touch-ups.

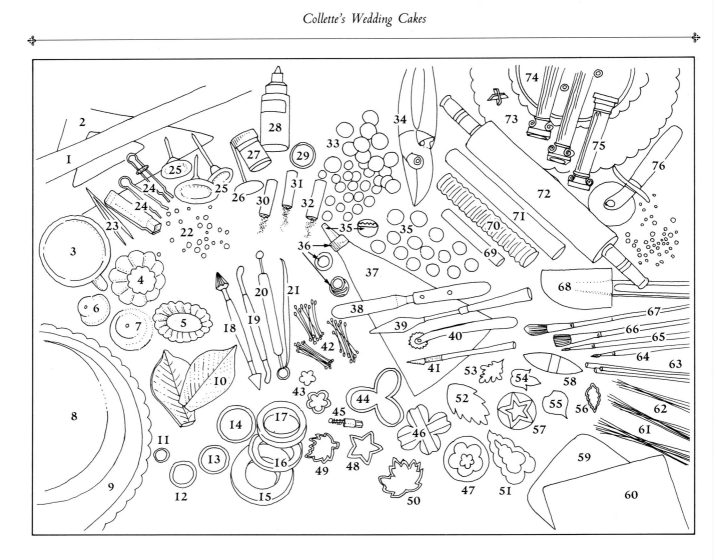

Equipment Pictured

1	Metal ruler	26	Flower nail	47	Flower cutter
2	Triangle	27	Paste food coloring	48	Star cutter
3	Cup of coffee, for	28	Liquid paste coloring	49–56	Leaf cutters
	late-night decorating	29–32	Silver, gold, purple, blue	57	Star cutter
4 & 5	Tart pans		nontoxic powdered colors	58	Lily cutter
6 & 7	Bell molds	33	Compound chocolate	59–60	Foam rubber
8	Styrofoam disk	34	Clippers	61	Cloth-covered wires
9	Turntable	35	Decorating tips	62	Bamboo skewers
10	Rubber leaf veiner	36	Couplers	63	Woooden dowels
11–14	Circle cutters	37	Pastry bag	64–67	Paintbrushes
15–17	Florist tape	38	Angled metal spatula	68	Rubber spatula
18	Trumpet flower tool	39	Palette knife	69	Plastic gum-paste rolling pin
19	Curved ball tool	40	Tracing wheel	70	Ridged rolling pin
20	Ball tool	41	X-acto knife	71	Wooden rolling pin
21	Veining tool	42	Stamens	72	Rolling pin
22	Dragées	43	Blossom cutters	73–74	Plastic separator plates
23	Tweezers	44	Tulip cutter	75	Columns
24	Crimpers	45	Small blossom plunger cutter	76	Pizza cutter
25	Lily nails	46	Dogwood cutter		

Glossary of Basic Tools

ALUMINUM FOIL: Indispensable when piping trumpet-shaped royal-icing flowers and for forming some gum-paste flowers.

CHOCOLATE COATING: Comes in disks in a variety of flavors and colors. Not a true chocolate; used for decorating in place of white, dark, or milk chocolate. (Do not use as a replacement for real chocolate in cake and icing recipes.) Also called summer coating because it doesn't melt in warm weather as easily as real chocolate. Available in candy- or cake-decorating stores.

CLOTH-COVERED WIRES: Available in white or green and a range of thicknesses, from #20 (the thickest) to #28 (the thinnest). Used for making stems for flowers and leaves made of gum paste or royal icing. Found in florist shops and cake-decorating stores.

COLUMNS: Available in various heights and styles. Made to fit tightly onto pegs on plastic separator plates, they add strength to the structure of a pillared cake. Found in cake-decorating stores.

COMPASS. A simple metal tool that holds a pencil or lead for drawing circles.

COUPLERS: Plastic couplers let you easily change tips on a pastry bag. The coupler fits inside the bag and the tip fits on top, secured by a threaded ring. All tips, except for very small and large ones, fit onto couplers. Large and small tips can be placed directly in the pastry bag, but you cannot change tips once you have filled the bag with icing.

CRIMPERS: Pronged tools for embossing designs in rolled fondant. Designed like tweezers, the ends of the two prongs form a two-sided pattern when you pinch fondant between them. Found in cake-decorating stores.

CUTTERS: Tools for making a variety of flowers and leaves in gum paste or modeling chocolate. Available in cake-decorating stores. You can also use cookie and biscuit cutters to make some flowers and ornaments.

DOWELS: $\frac{1}{4}$-inch-thick wooden dowels, used for supporting tiered cakes, can be bought at hardware or cake-decorating stores.

DRAGÉES: Silver or gold candy balls that add sparkle to cakes. They are nontoxic, but the Food & Drug Administration recommends that they be used for decoration only. Gold dragées come in 2 sizes: tiny seeds and $\frac{3}{16}$ inch. Silver dragées come in 6 sizes: tiny seeds; $\frac{1}{8}$-, $\frac{3}{16}$-, $\frac{1}{4}$-, and $\frac{3}{8}$-inch balls; and $\frac{1}{2}$-inch-long ovals. At this writing, dragées are unavailable in California. They can be purchased at the Chocolate Gallery (see page 182).

FLORIST'S TAPE: Used to cover wires and to bind flowers and leaves together. Available in white, brown, and green from florist shops and cake-decorating suppliers.

FLOWER NAILS: Flat or cupped supports on which flowers are piped. Available in cake-decorating stores.

FOAMCORE BOARD: A thin piece of Styrofoam sandwiched between 2 pieces of thin white cardboard. Used to make bases and to support tiers. Much stronger than corrugated cardboard and does not bend as easily. Easy to cut with an X-acto knife. Available at craft and art-supply stores.

FOOD COLORING: Comes in several forms: paste, liquid, liquid paste, and powder. Paste is the most versatile. The color is highly concentrated; a little dab on the end of a toothpick is usually all you need to make a pastel color. Found in cake-decorating supply stores.

Liquid food colors, commonly found in the grocery, sometimes come in handy; however, to achieve a dark color you must add large amounts, which will thin the icing and make piping difficult. Liquid paste, found in cake-decorating stores, is highly concentrated but thinner than paste.

Powdered food colors are used for metallic and iridescent effects or to create very deep colors. Flowers can be dusted with powder to make them look more realistic. Powdered colors can also be made into paint by adding a few drops of lemon extract. At this writing, the Food & Drug Administration considers metallic powders to be inedible, although they are nontoxic. They should be used for decoration only. Available at the Chocolate Gallery (see page 182).

GLUCOSE: A thicker version of corn syrup, used for making rolled fondant. Available in cake-decorating stores.

GLYCERINE: A thick, sweet syrup used to keep fondant soft and pliable. It can also be used for thinning paste coloring if it becomes too thick. Available in cake-decorating stores.

GUM-PASTE TOOLS: A variety of gum-paste modeling tools can be found at cake-decorating stores. See the section on gum paste (page 155).

HEAVY-DUTY MIXER: For the occasional baker, a regular upright mixer is fine, but if you plan to do a substantial amount of decorating you need a heavy-duty mixer. Handheld mixers tend to burn out and are not very efficient.

HOT-GLUE GUN: This gun-shaped tool melts plastic glue sticks to apply melted glue, a strong adhesive for Styrofoam or foamcore. You can buy a glue gun at craft or hardware stores.

PAINTBRUSHES: Flat or round, soft paintbrushes and pastry brushes come in handy in almost every aspect of decorating. Natural-hair brushes are recommended over synthetic brushes.

PASTA MACHINE: Small and relatively inexpensive pasta machines have a handcrank, but you can convert them into motorized machines to enable you to work with both hands. Very helpful for rolling out uniformly thick strips of gum paste or modeling chocolate to make ribbons, flowers, or leaves.

PASTRY BAGS: The best type of bag is made of lightweight polyester. Cloth bags are bulky and hard to clean, and disposable plastic bags break easily. Buy a few bags and use some only for royal icing and others only for buttercream. The fat from the buttercream will break down royal icing, even if the bag is thoroughly cleaned. I find the 10-inch bag the easiest size to work with; larger bags tend to tire the hands quickly.

PIZZA CUTTER: Handy for trimming rolled fondant or for cutting strips of gum paste or modeling chocolate.

PLASTIC CUTTING BOARD: I use plastic boards to roll out gum paste. You can also use less expensive plastic place mats.

PLASTIC WRAP: For wrapping and storing gum paste and modeling chocolate.

PRUNING SHEARS: For trimming wooden dowels.

ROLLING PIN: A large one is essential for rolling out fondant; use a small wooden or plastic one for rolling out gum paste.

RULER: A metal ruler is more durable than a plastic one, which is easily cut or knicked. An 18-inch length is the most versatile, although smaller rulers also come in handy.

SCISSORS: Large and small sharp scissors are a necessity for cutting paper, ribbons, etc.

SEPARATOR PLATES: Plastic plates made specifically for cakes come in a wide variety of sizes. Each plate has four pegs that snap into the tops and bottoms of plastic columns to secure the tiers.

SPATULA: An assortment of spatulas is an absolute necessity for baking and decorating — rubber for scraping bowls of batter or icing, and stainless steel for spreading and smoothing icing. The one I use most is an 8-inch angled spatula. A plastic or stainless-steel icing smoother is also a great aid when icing large cakes. These are all found in cake-decorating stores. A palette knife is also useful for releasing run-in sugar decorations from wax paper.

STAMENS: These can be found in cake-decorating stores or florist shops. A stamen consists of a thin piece of stiff thread with a tiny ball on each end. The thread is cut in half, and the ends are inserted into the center of a royal-icing or gum-paste flower. They come in a variety of colors and sizes and are not edible.

STYROFOAM: Found in craft or cake-decorating stores. Essential for making bouquets, beveled layers, and display cakes. See the section on Styrofoam (page 174).

TIPS: There are hundreds of decorating tips to choose from. Beginners may want to purchase a basic set and buy additional tips as needed. I use small round tips more than any others. PME brand tips are seamless and much more expensive than ordinary tips with seams (around $5.00, as opposed to 59¢), but for certain techniques, such as stringwork, they are a must. Tips with seams tend to force icing out in spirals; seamless tips force the icing in smooth straight lines. I suggest that you buy a few of the more expensive tips in sizes #0, #1, #1.5, #2, and #3.

Round tips range in size from #00 through #12 to even larger, such as 1A and 2A. Star tips are numbered from #13 to #35, but there are also larger ones. Leaf tips number #65S through #70 and #352. Larger leaf tips are #326, #355, #112, #113, #114, and #115. Rose-petal tips range from #101S through #104, then #124 to #127, and curved rose tips number #60, #61, #121, #122, and #123. Ribbon tips range from #44 through #48, and larger ribbons are #1D and 2B. Tips #79, #80, and #81 make mums and lilies of the valley. There are also many specialty tips.

TOOTHPICKS: Round toothpicks can be tinted green with liquid food coloring to make flower stems. They are also useful for adding paste colors to icing, embossing fondant, and marking icing. Bamboo skewers can also be used when longer stems are needed.

TRACING WHEEL: Used for embossing quilt designs on rolled fondant. Available in sewing stores. Cake-decorating stores also carry a tracing wheel with two interchangeable wheels, one with teeth and one that makes a zigzag pattern. A pastry wheel will also create a zigzag effect.

TURNTABLE: Invaluable for working your way around a cake. Cake-decorating stores sell turntables on stands, but you don't have to buy an expensive model; plastic ones carried by most hardware stores designed for storing spices are fine and will support very heavy cakes.

TWEEZERS: Most helpful for picking up and positioning dragées, stamens, or flowers.

VEINERS: Plastic or rubber molds that emboss veins in gum-paste flowers and leaves.

WAX PAPER: Used when making royal-icing flowers and for piping removable royal-icing decorations.

X-ACTO KNIFE: I constantly use an X-acto knife with a long pointed blade (#11). The knife has a thin metal handle and a blade that screws in and can be changed easily. You will need a lot of extra blades because they tend to dull quickly. They can be found at craft and art-supply stores.

Sources for Decorating Supplies

Broadway Panhandler
520 Broadway
New York, NY 10012
212-966-3434

Country Kitchen
3225 Wells Street
Fort Wayne, IN 46808
219-482-4835

Creative Cutters
561 Edward Avenue, Units 1 & 2
Richmond Hill, Ontario
Canada L4C 9W6
905-883-5638
Fax: 905-770-3091

Offray Ribbon
800-344-5533 (U.S.)
800-363-3729 (Canada)

The Cake Plate
104 11th N.E.
East Wenatchee, WA 98801
509-884-1549

The Chocolate Gallery
56 West 22nd Street
New York, NY 10010
212-675-CAKE

Parrish's Cake Decorating Supplies, Inc.
225 West 146th Street
Gardena, CA 90248
310-324-CAKE
Fax: 310-324-8277

Wilton Industries
2240 West 75th Street
Woodridge, IL 60517
708-963-7100

Index